THE PATHS WE TAKE

Words and Images showing the extraordinary world in which we live

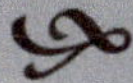

Photography and Poetry by
Kerrie Flanagan & Suzette McIntyre
featuring
the award winning art
of our second juried Words & Images Competition

Contents

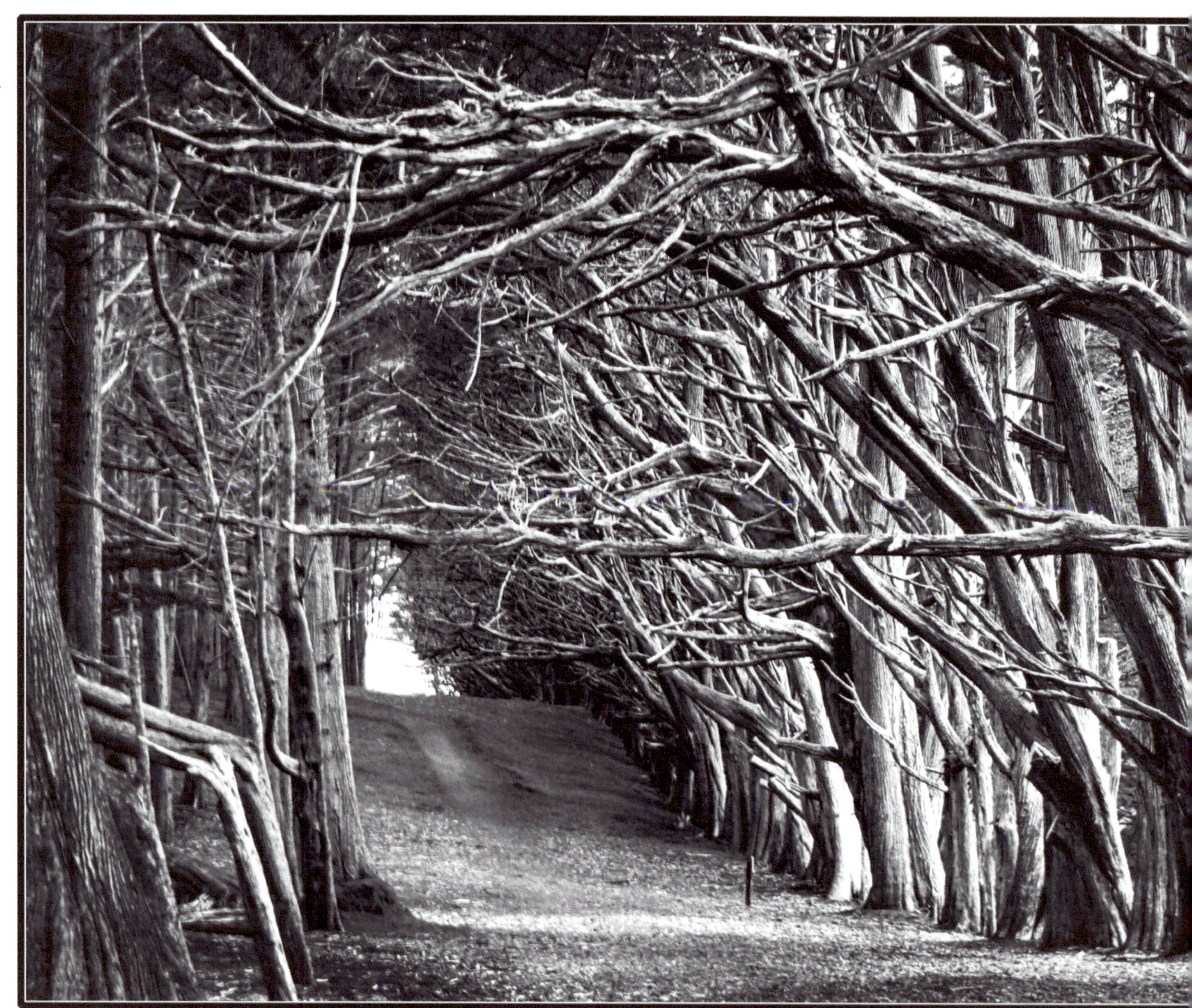

Just Beyond

Portal
To a new land
Where magic awaits you
One step at a time; trust the trees
Be brave

❧

Kerrie Flanagan

MOVING FORWARD

Empty your hands of yesterday
and you can grasp what lies ahead.

~Suzette

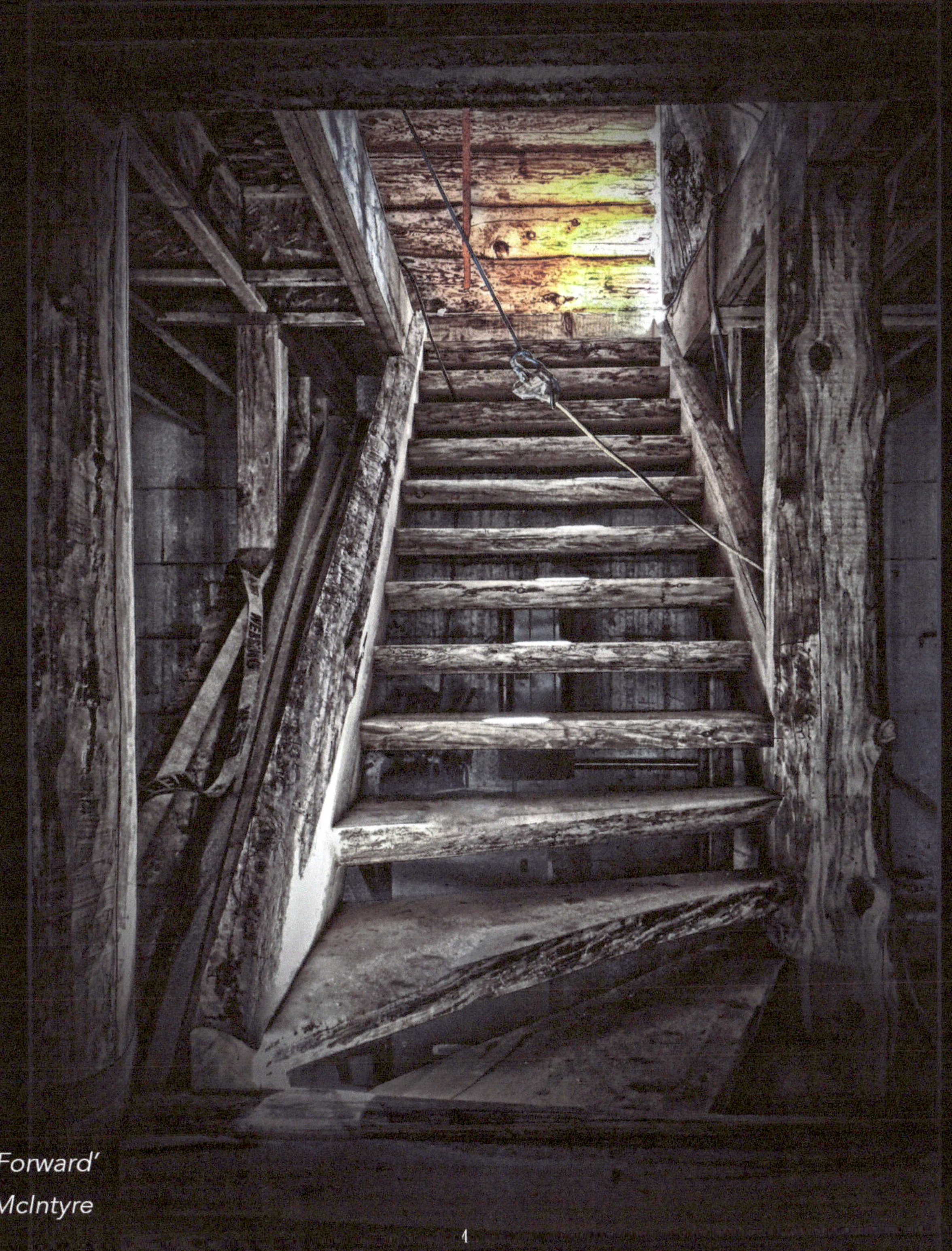

'Moving Forward'
Suzette McIntyre

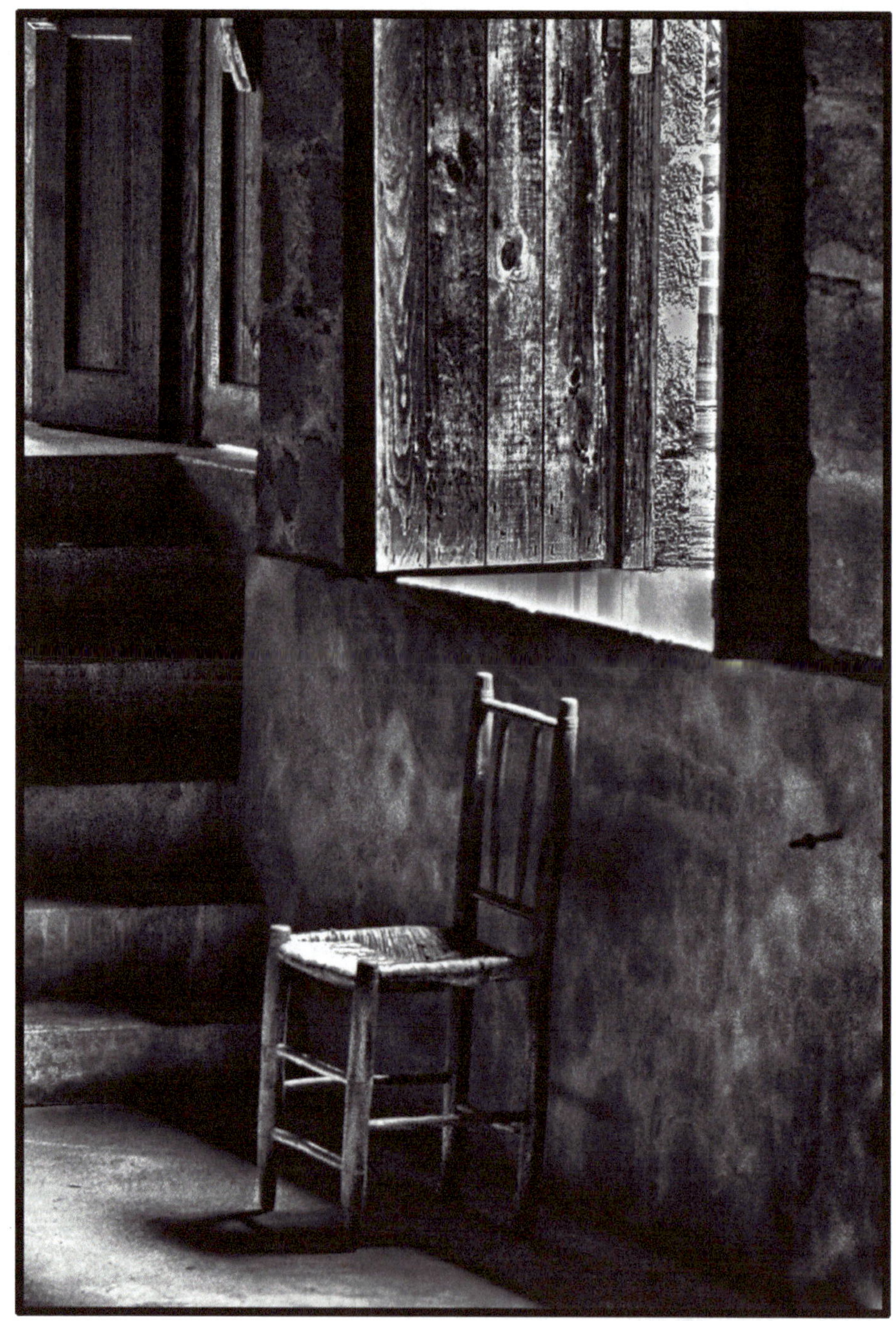

'Waiting'   Suzette McIntyre

Everything evolves in its own time.
Trust the wait.

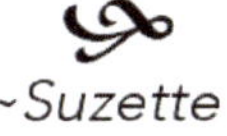

~Suzette

Long Ago

The past rises up
Forgotten dreams and memories
Stir lost emotions

ℒ

Kerrie Flanagan

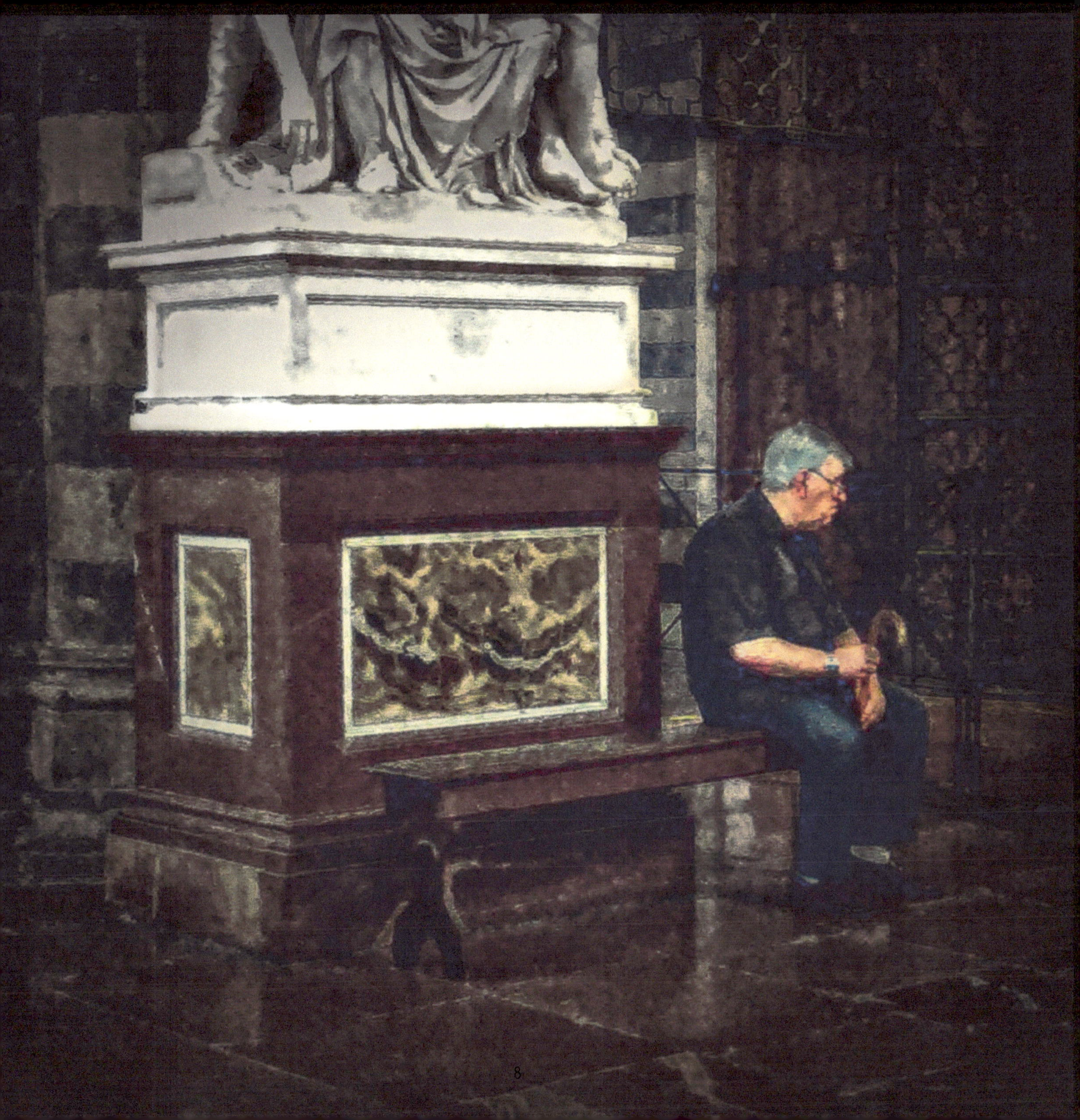

Hope

*It's time
Time to look up
Your future awaits
With each brave step your past fades back
New life*

Kerrie Flanagan

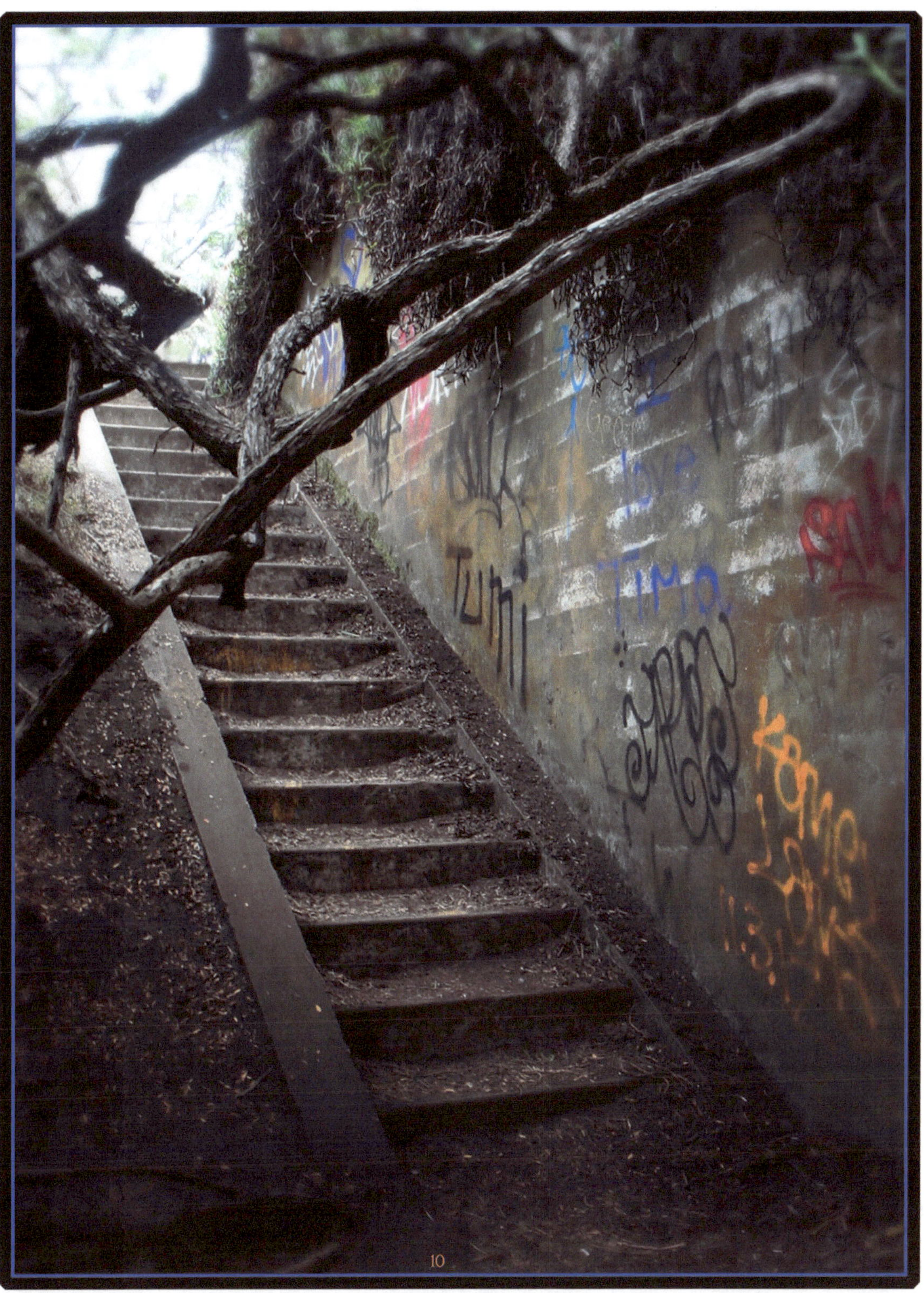

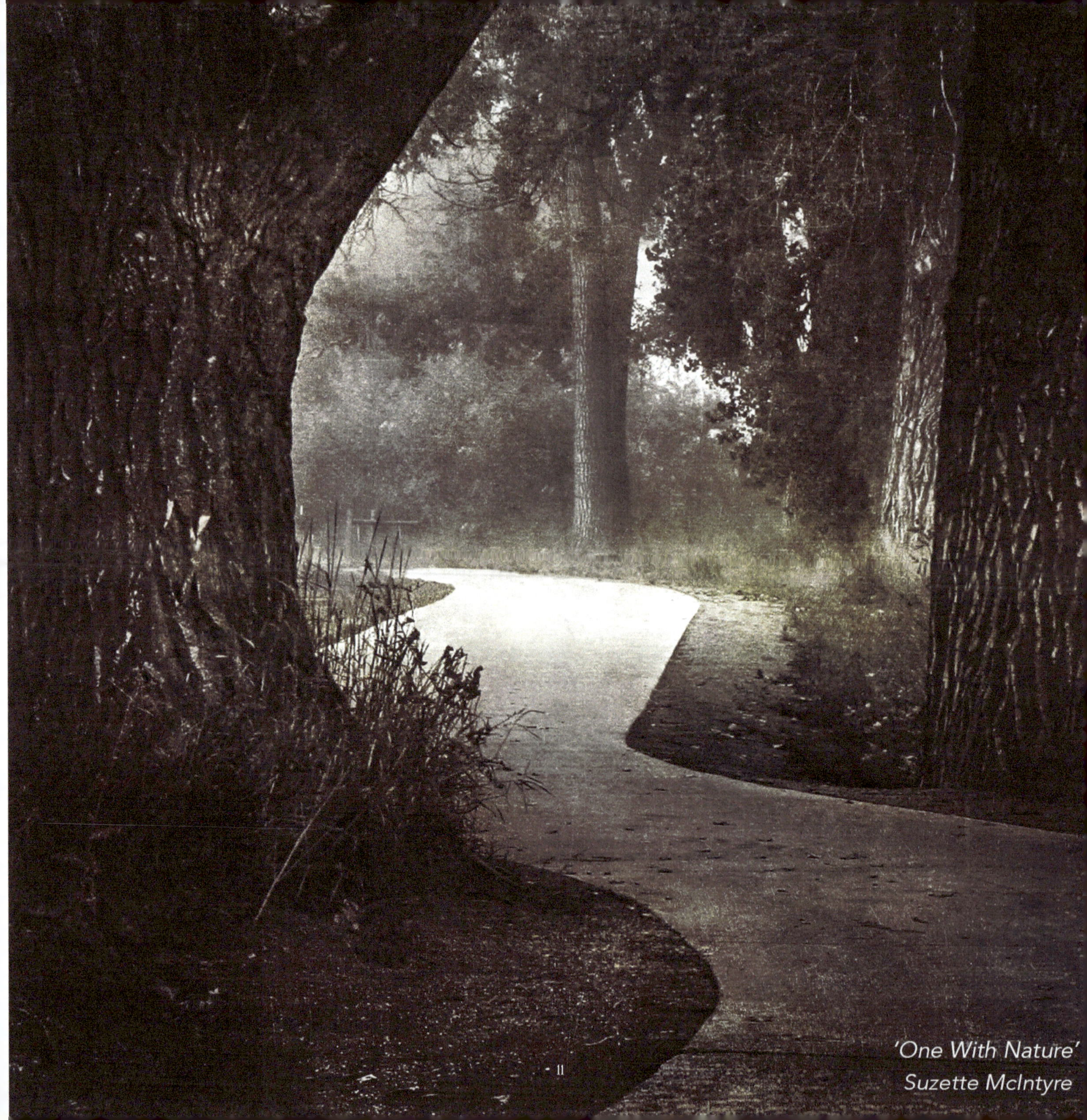

'One With Nature'
Suzette McIntyre

One With Nature

In an early run
along a deep winding path
I learned the hawk's cry.

~Suzette

Out beyond ideas of
wrongdoing and rightdoing
there is is field.

I'll meet you there.

~Rumi

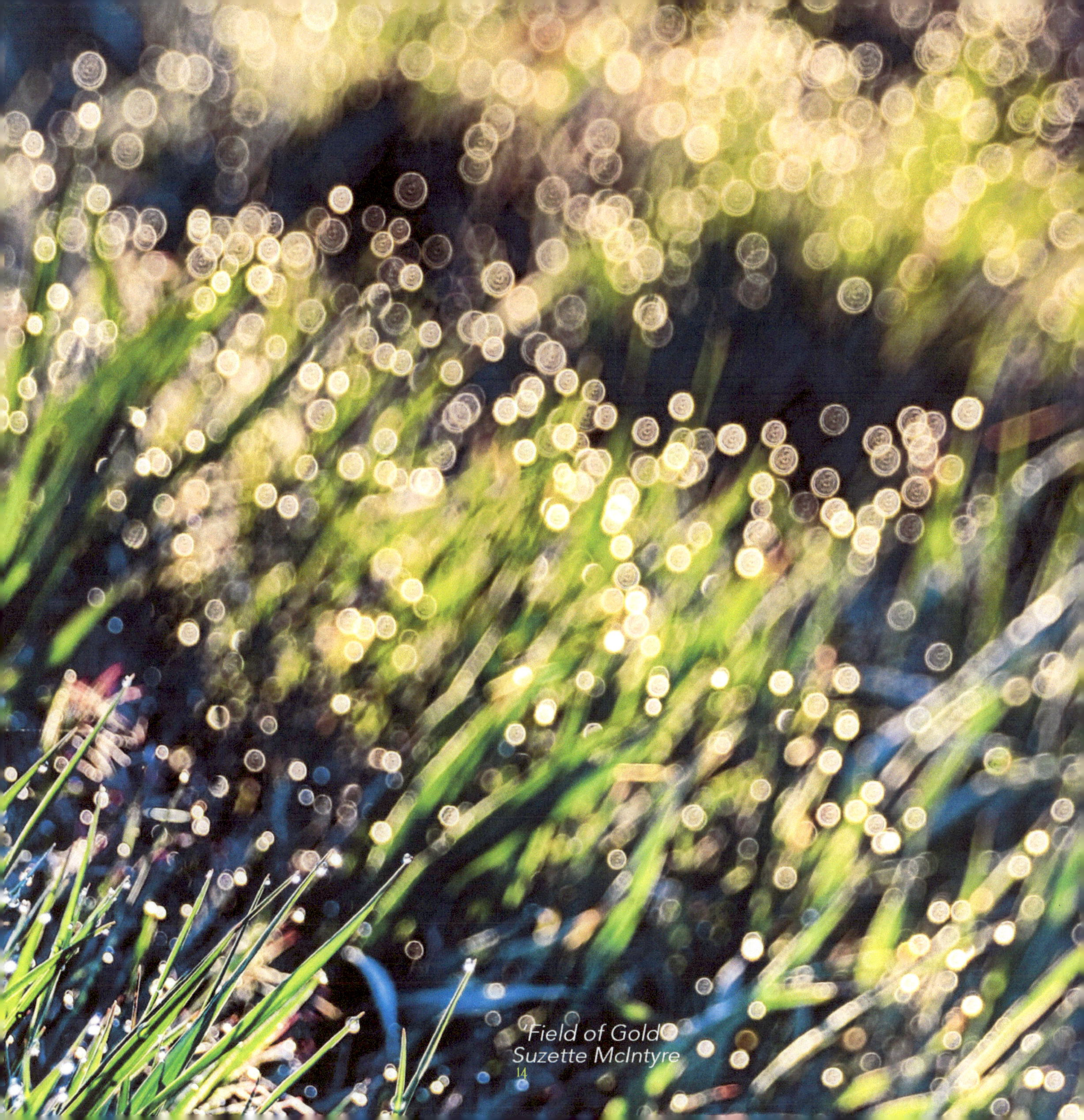

'Field of Gold'
Suzette McIntyre

Escape

The words
Come together
Gently pulling me in
And opening up a new world
Sheer bliss

Kerrie Flanagan

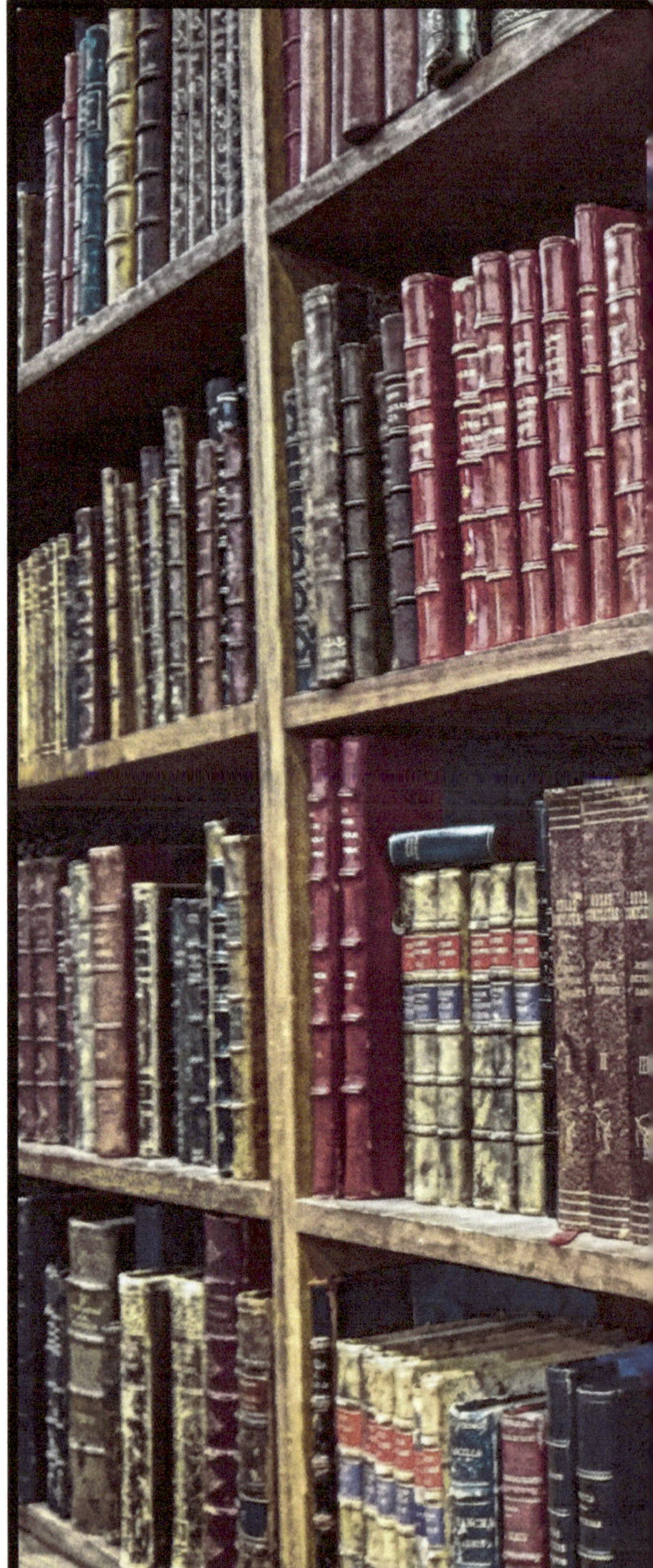

15

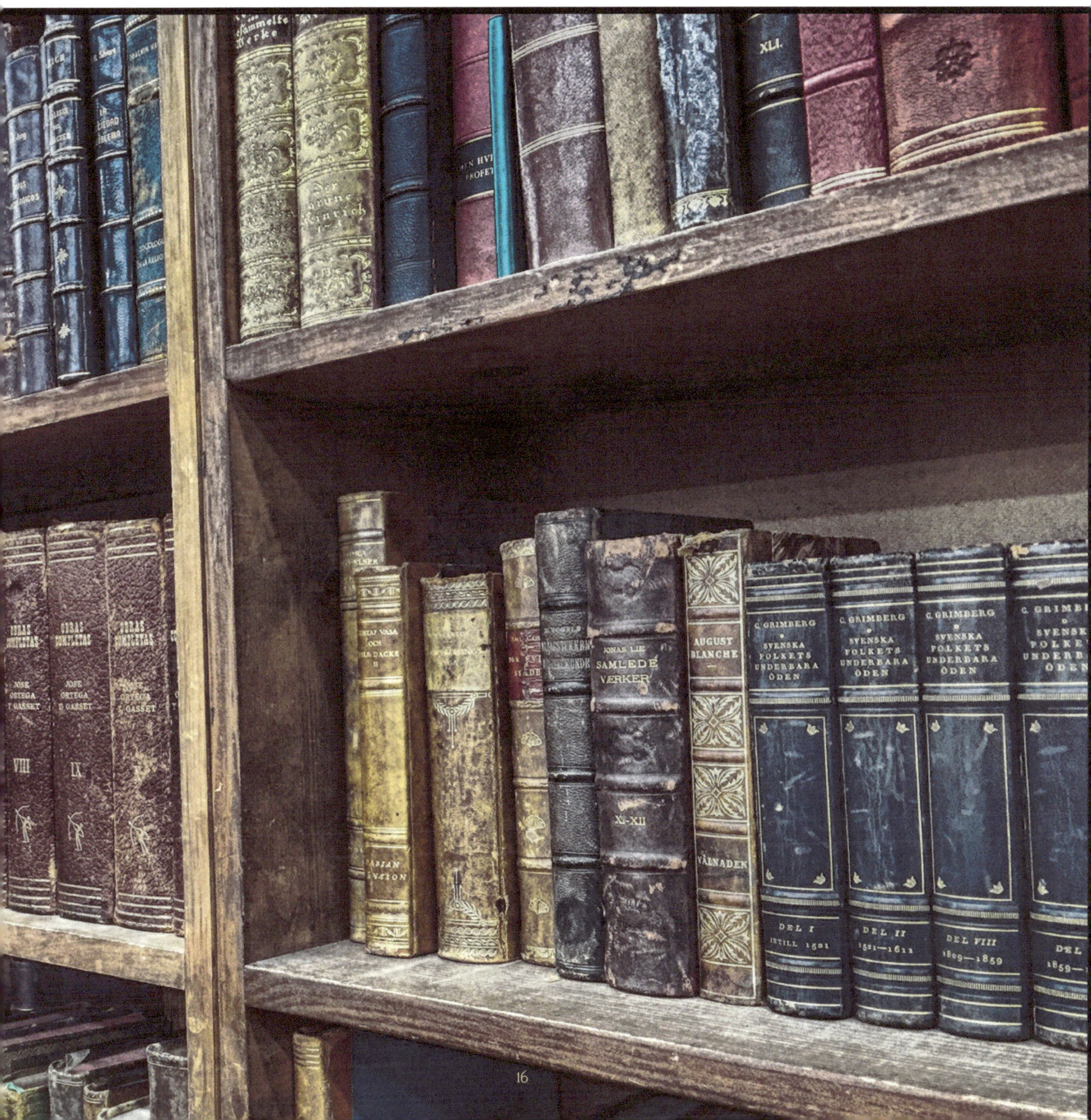

To the Top

Smiling
Wishing others well
as she passes.
Determination fuels her
until she is finally there.
Success!
The view is amazing.

﹆

Kerrie Flanagan

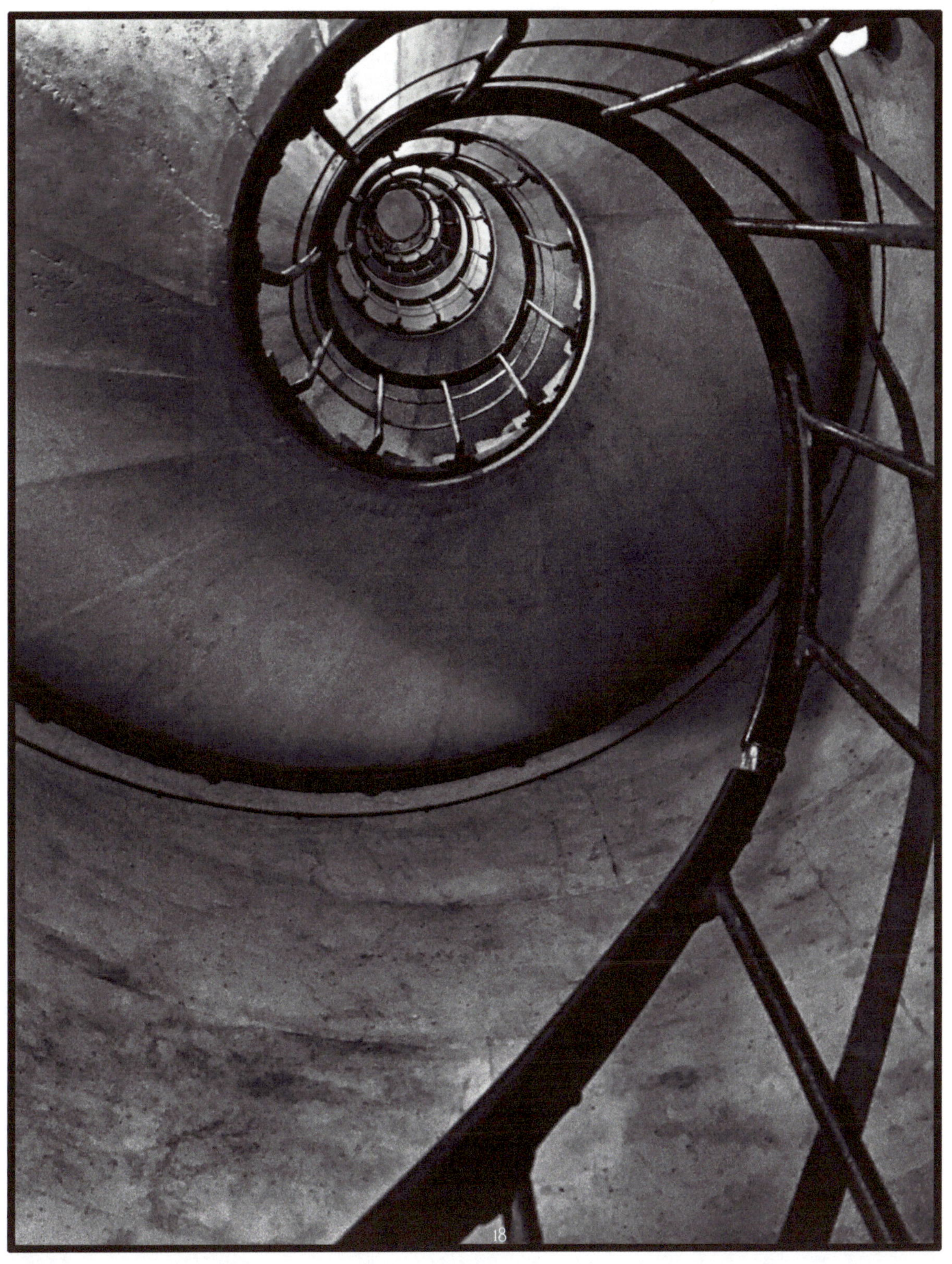

Sometimes I can hear you in the midnight sky
Whispering what might have been.

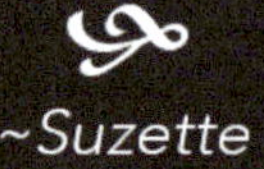

~Suzette

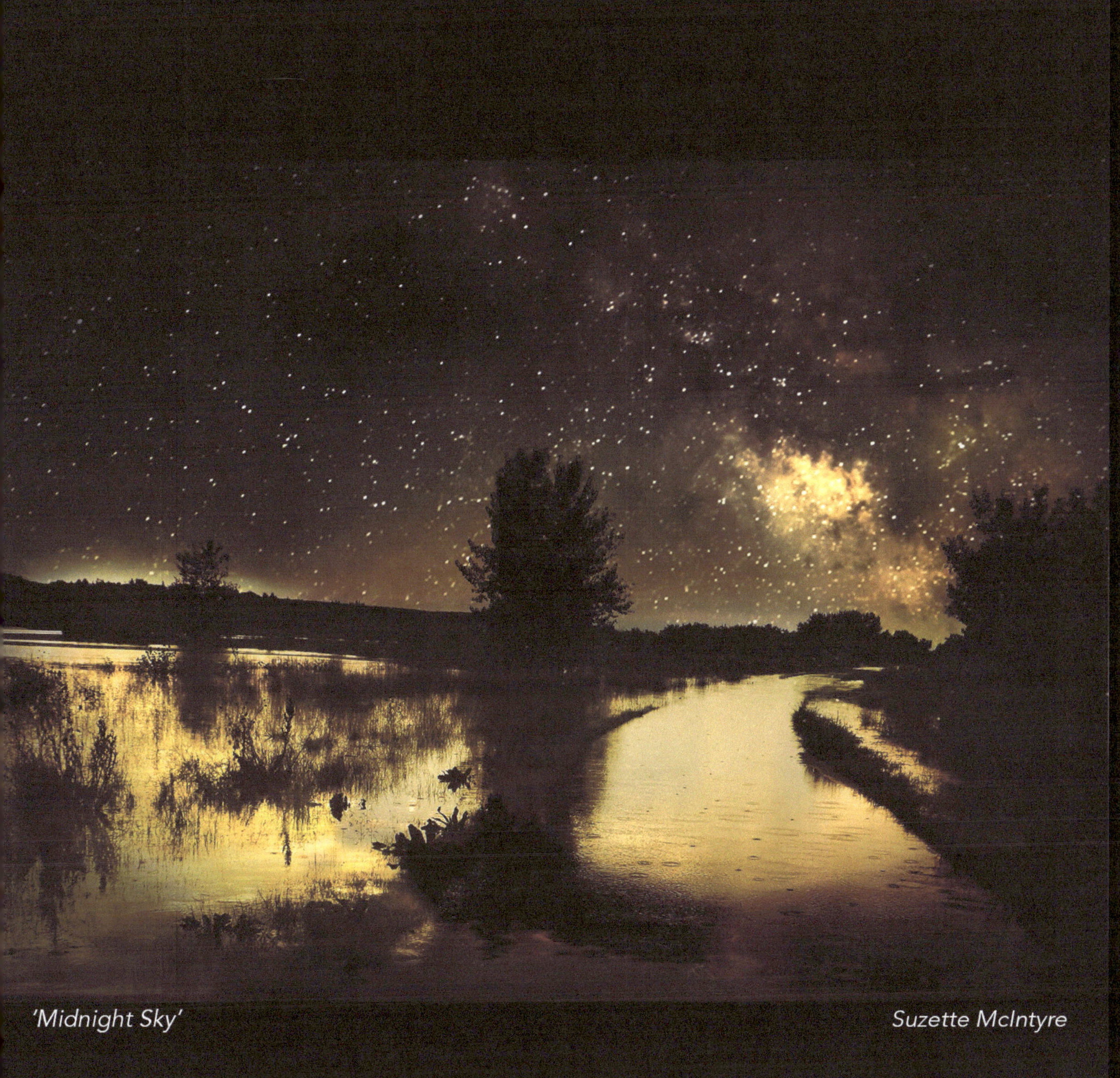

'Midnight Sky'
Suzette McIntyre

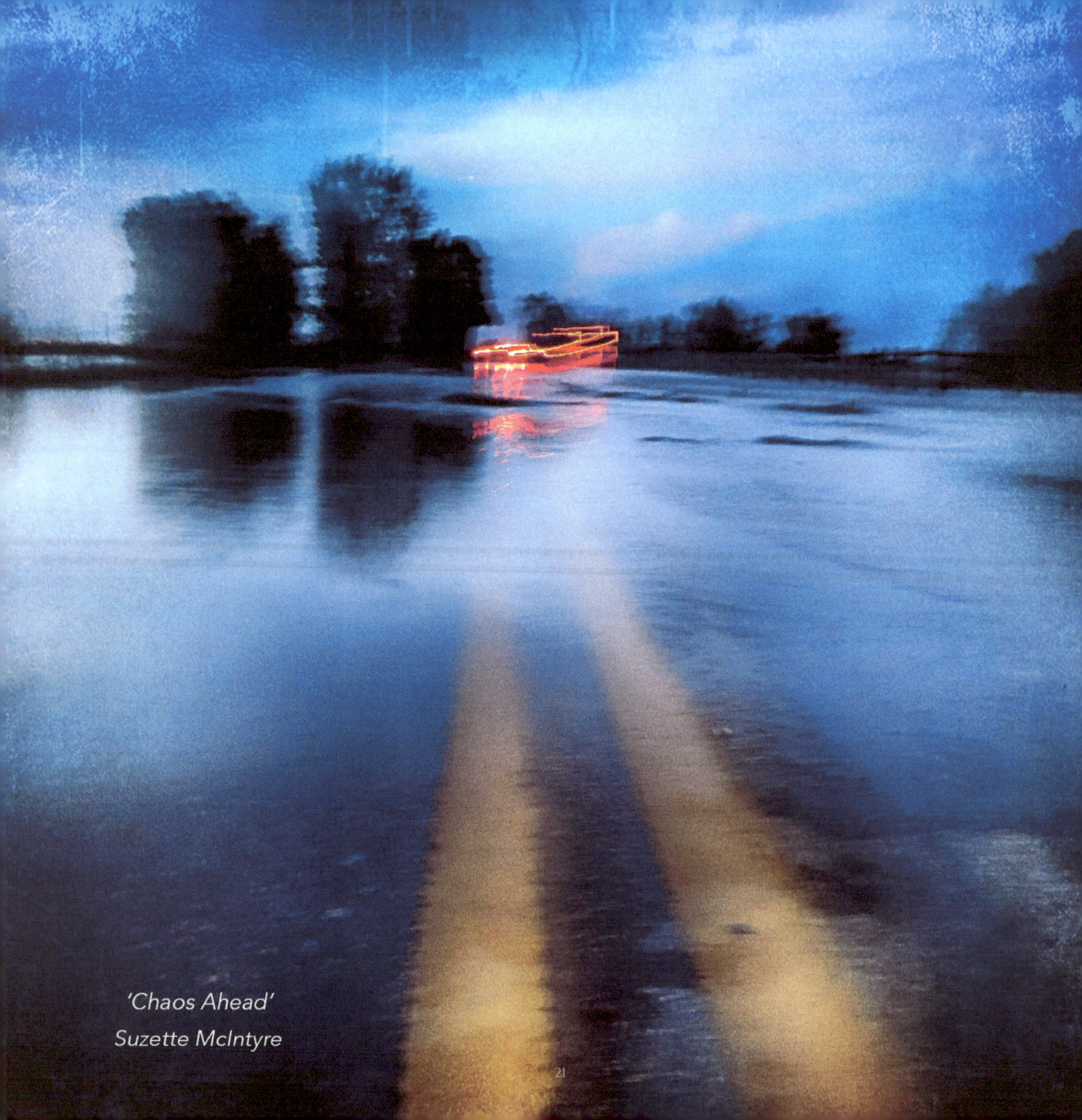

'Chaos Ahead'
Suzette McIntyre

I cannot go back, I can only move forward
...and you are not there.

~Suzette

Cleansing

Regret, sorrow, remorse--
All washing away
with each
tiny
raindrop

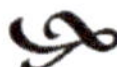

Kerrie Flanagan

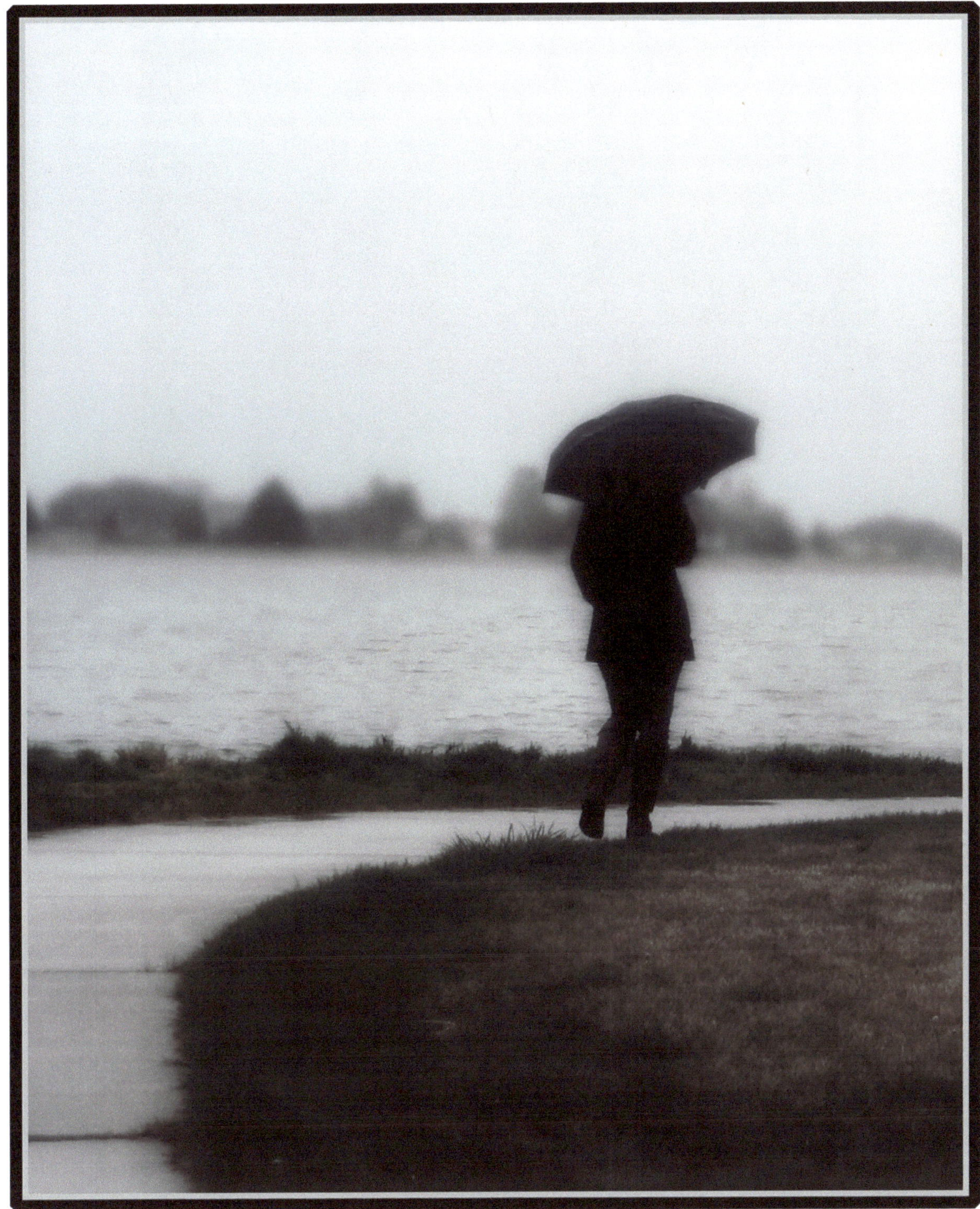

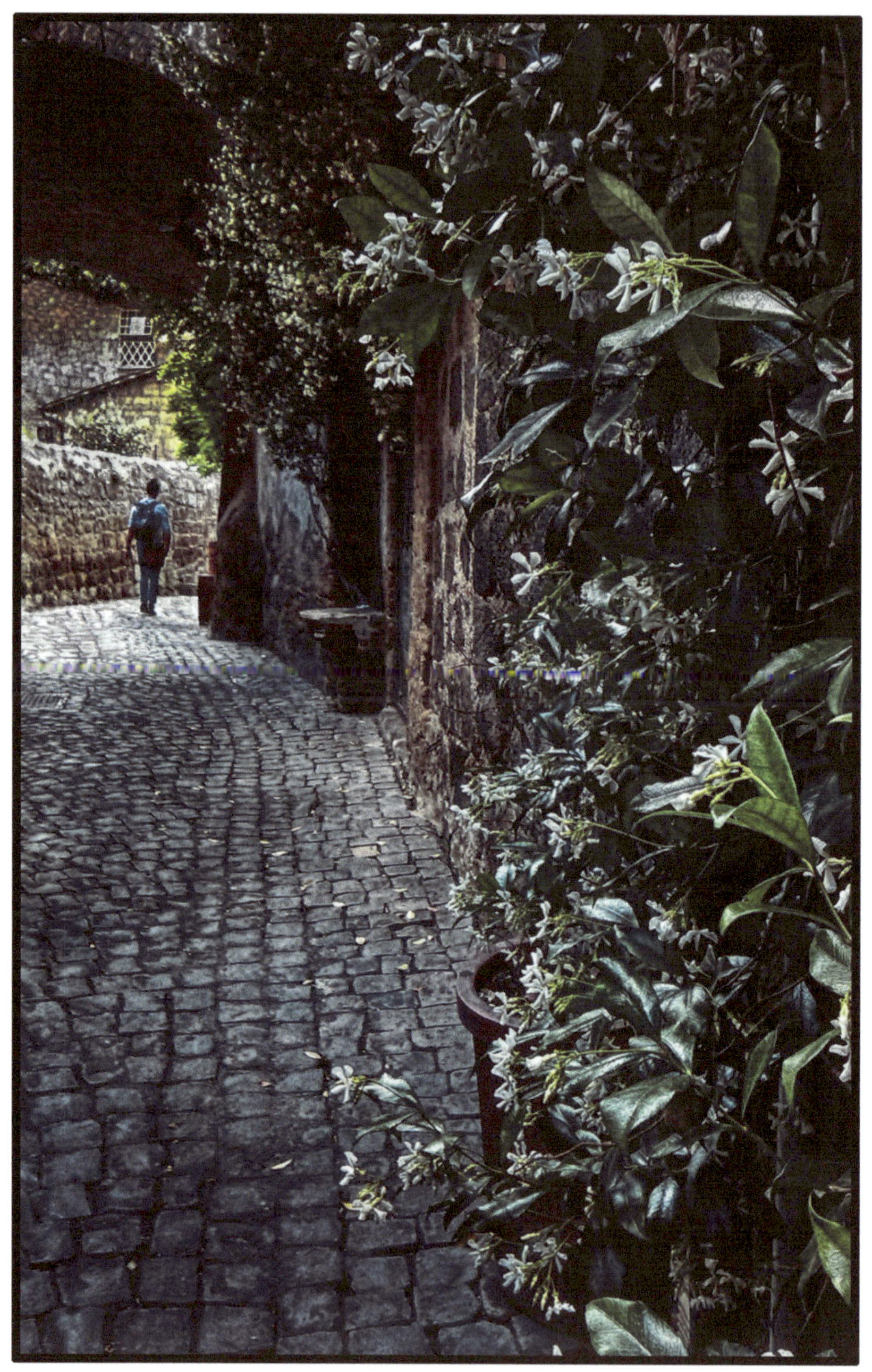

New Beginning

No more looking back!
Keeping my face to the sun
toward a bright future.

&

Kerrie Flanagan

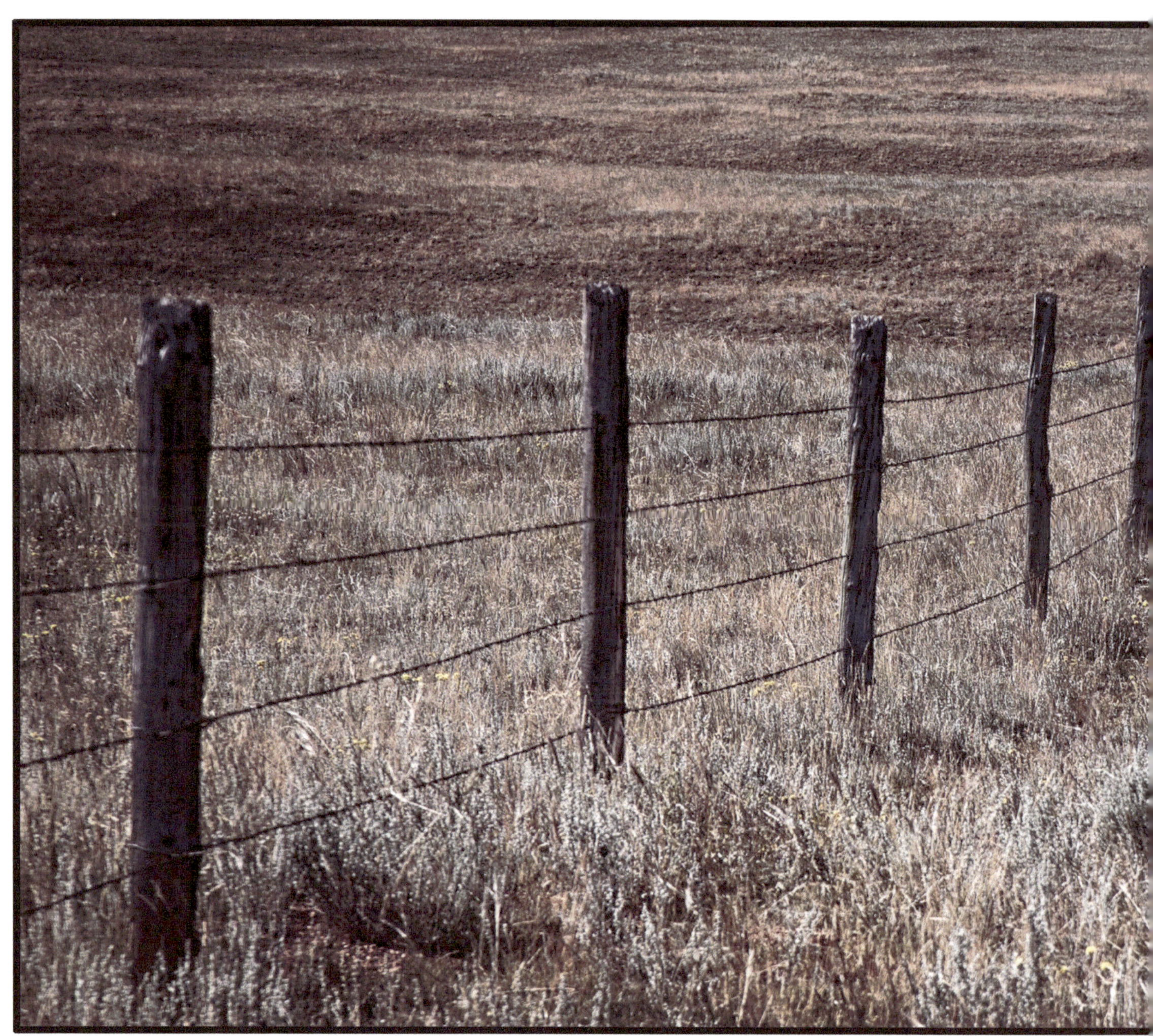

'BEYOND THE PATH'
Suzette McIntyre

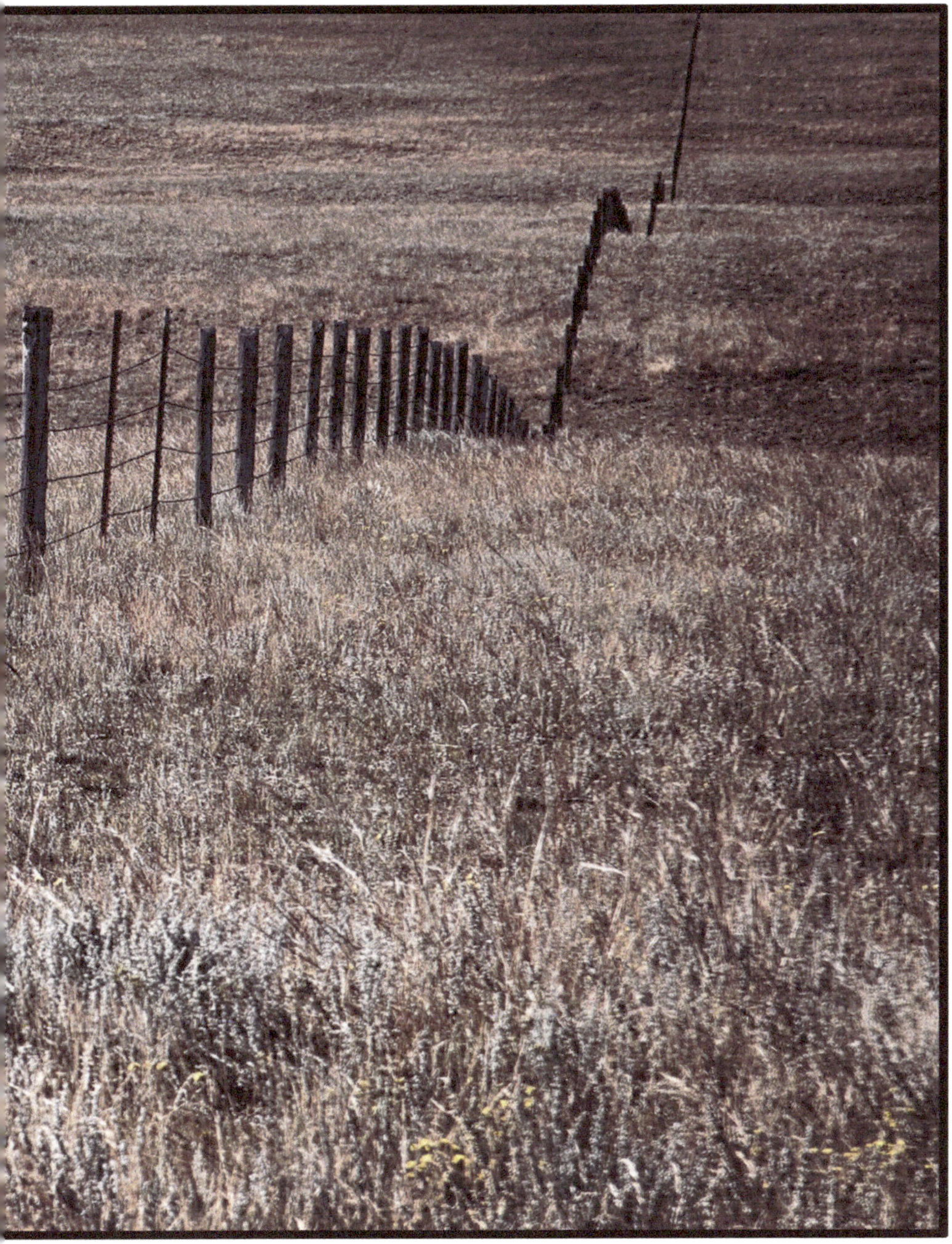

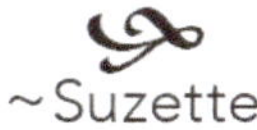

Step outside the
prison of your mind
and discover
what lies beyond.

~Suzette

Detachment

How far can one go
before we give up
and
turn
away?

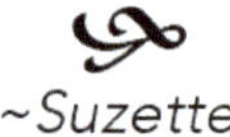

~Suzette

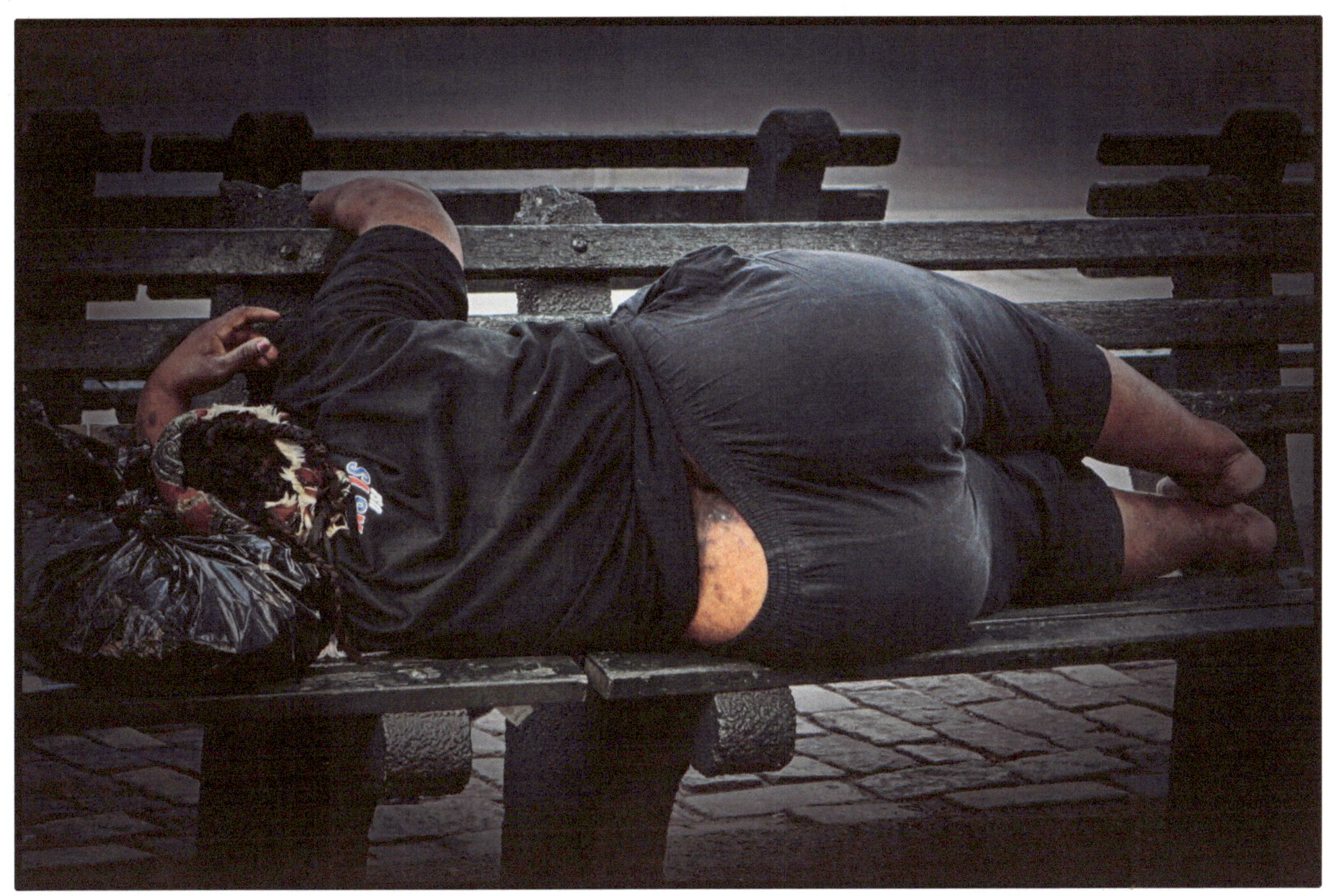

'Turning Away'   *Suzette McIntyre*

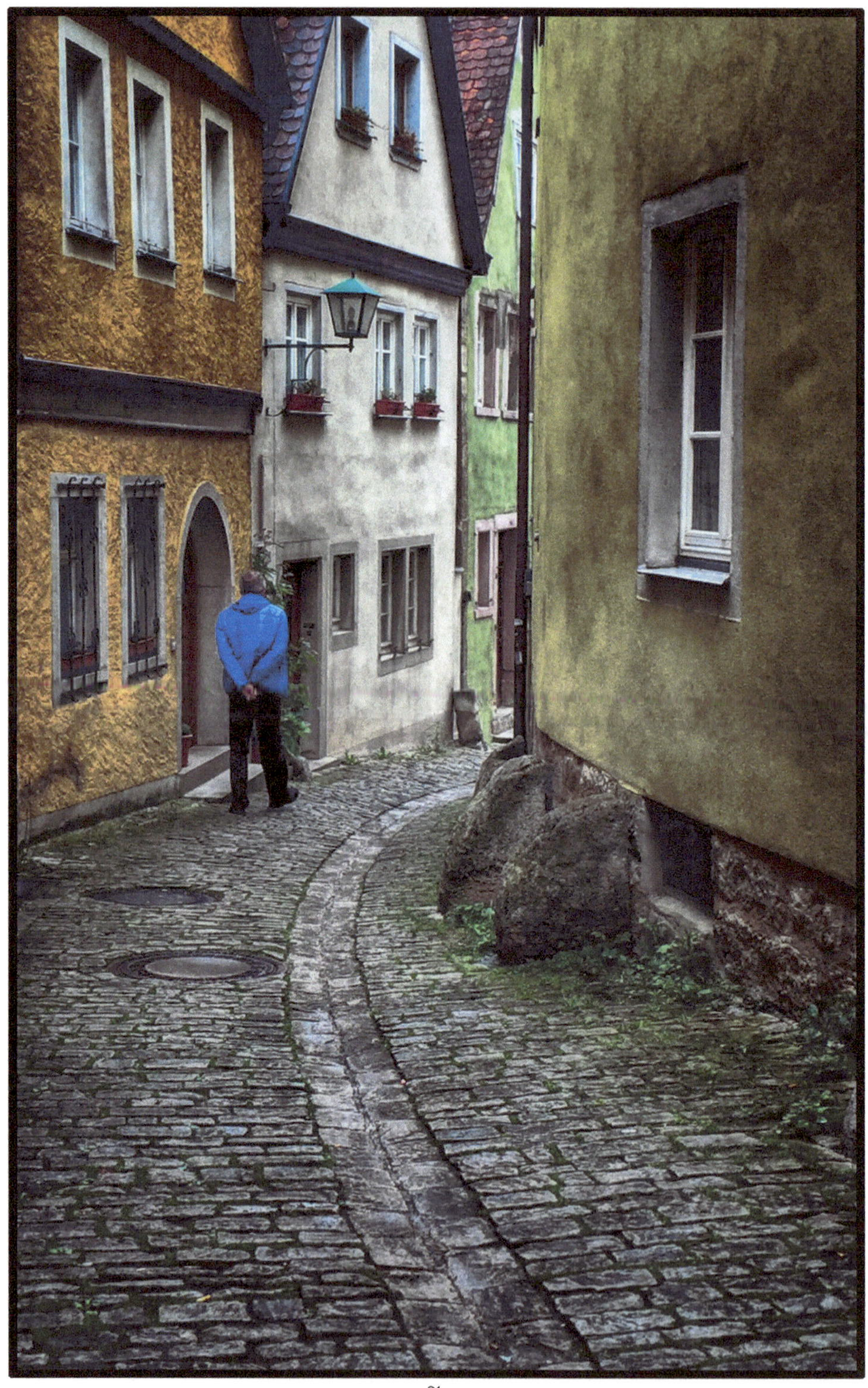

Contemplation

Quiet Street,
thoughts come to life,
filled with memories and dreams.
Slowly they fade away
when reality surfaces
again…

જી

Kerrie Flanagan

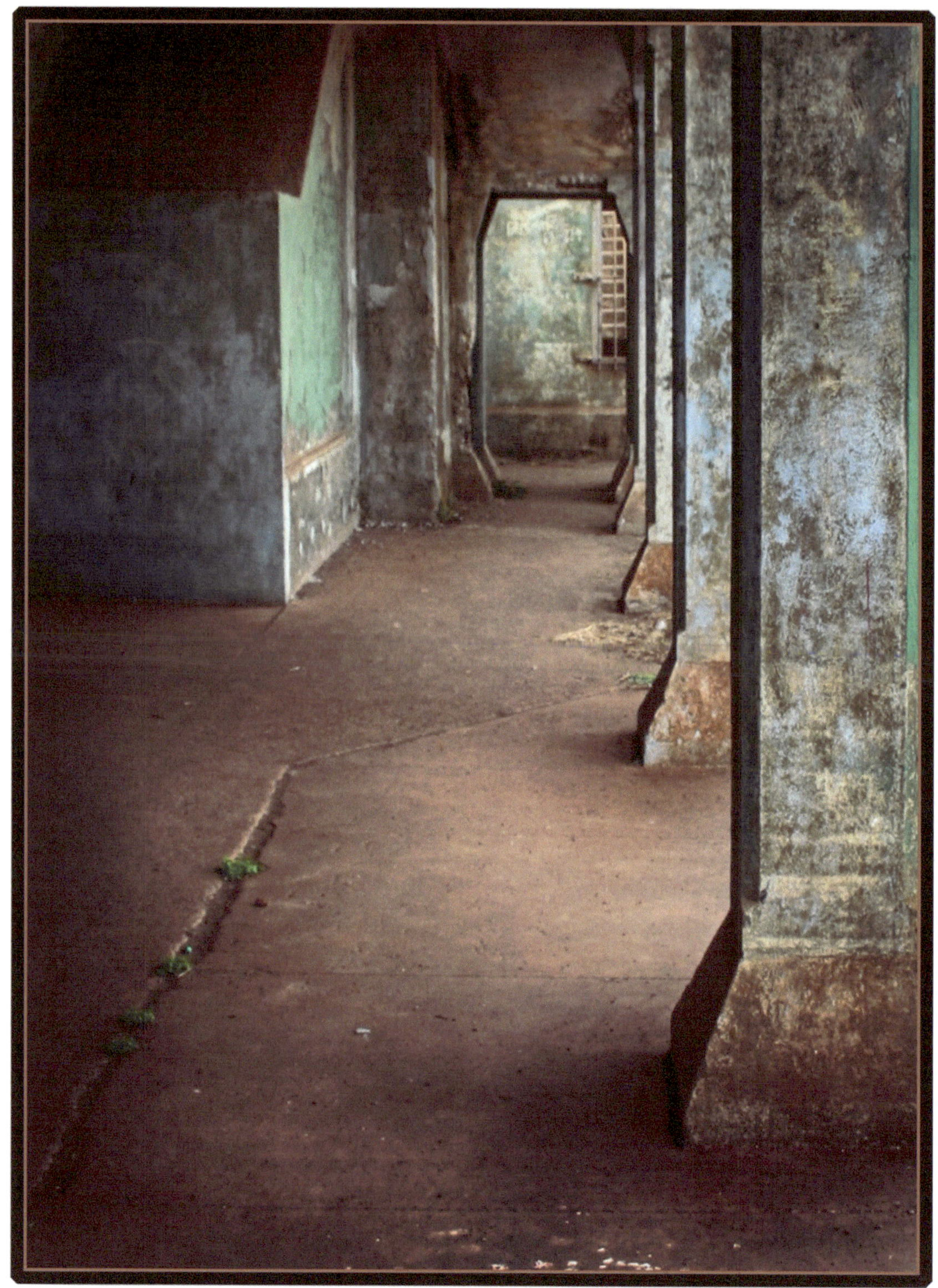

Quiet Refuge

Refuge
High on a hill
Overlooking the sea
Offered protection long ago
Now quiet

Kerrie Flanagan

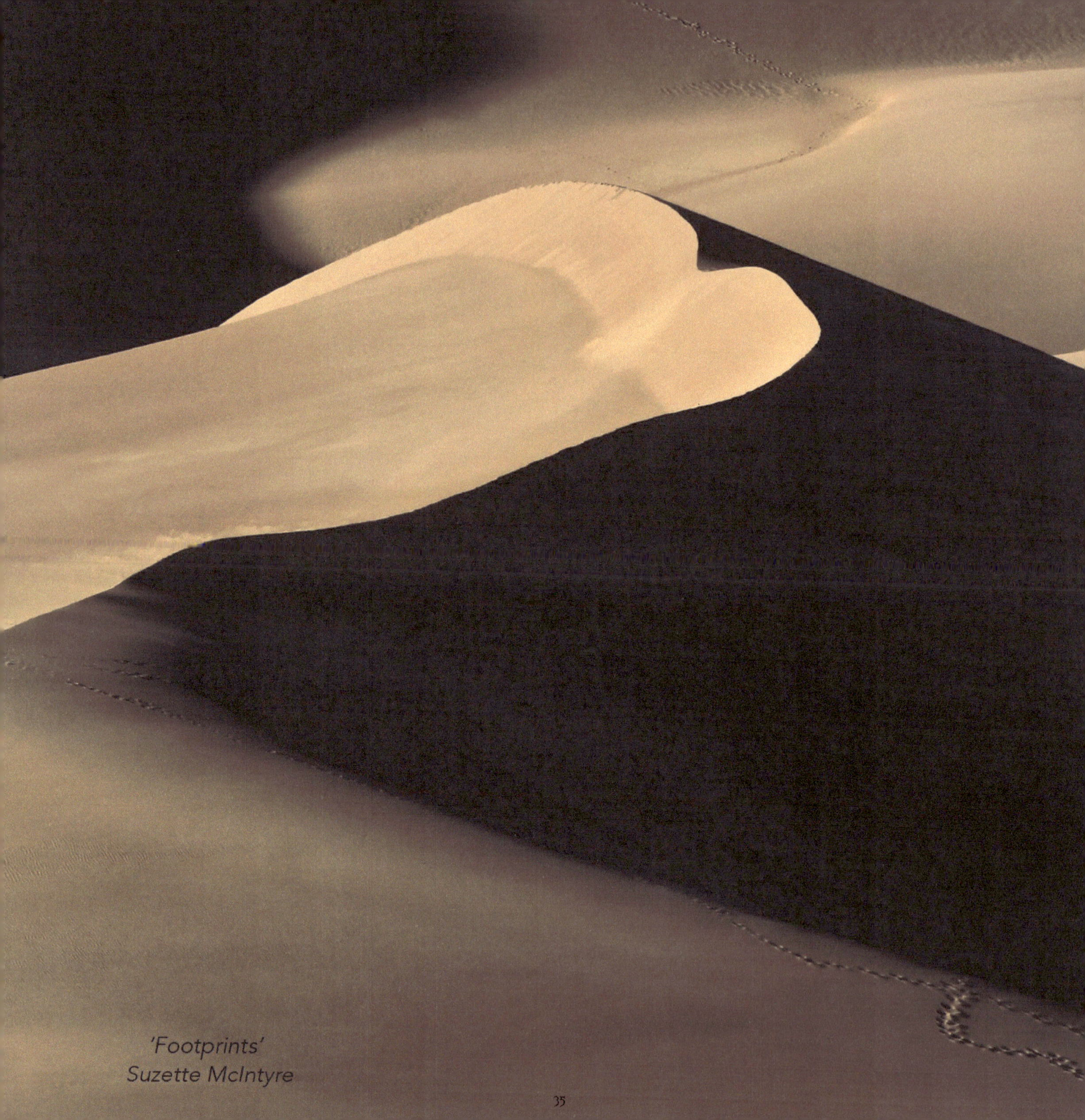

'Footprints'
Suzette McIntyre

Navigator

The maps are clear – my navigation,
I think, is not. I have lost
My point of reference; I spin
As wildly as a compass rose set askew.
Even dizzy, though, my eyes still follow
The lines, the beautifully painted lines,
The rises and hollows, the paths,
The mountains and the creeks laid out
So plainly before me - I read the map
On your face, in your words,
In the creases of your many-folded letters,
And I can see the end,
See every end, see every destination
And its certain course – it is my own
Marker which is lost, my own
Footprints I cannot find upon the page.

Cassondra Windwalker
First Place/Poetry

Immigrant

New customs,
new surroundings.
Rising above the stares
the challenges
the hardships.
Seeking what everyone wants;
what everyone deserves--
acceptance.

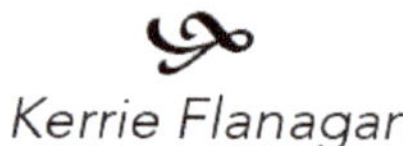

Kerrie Flanagan

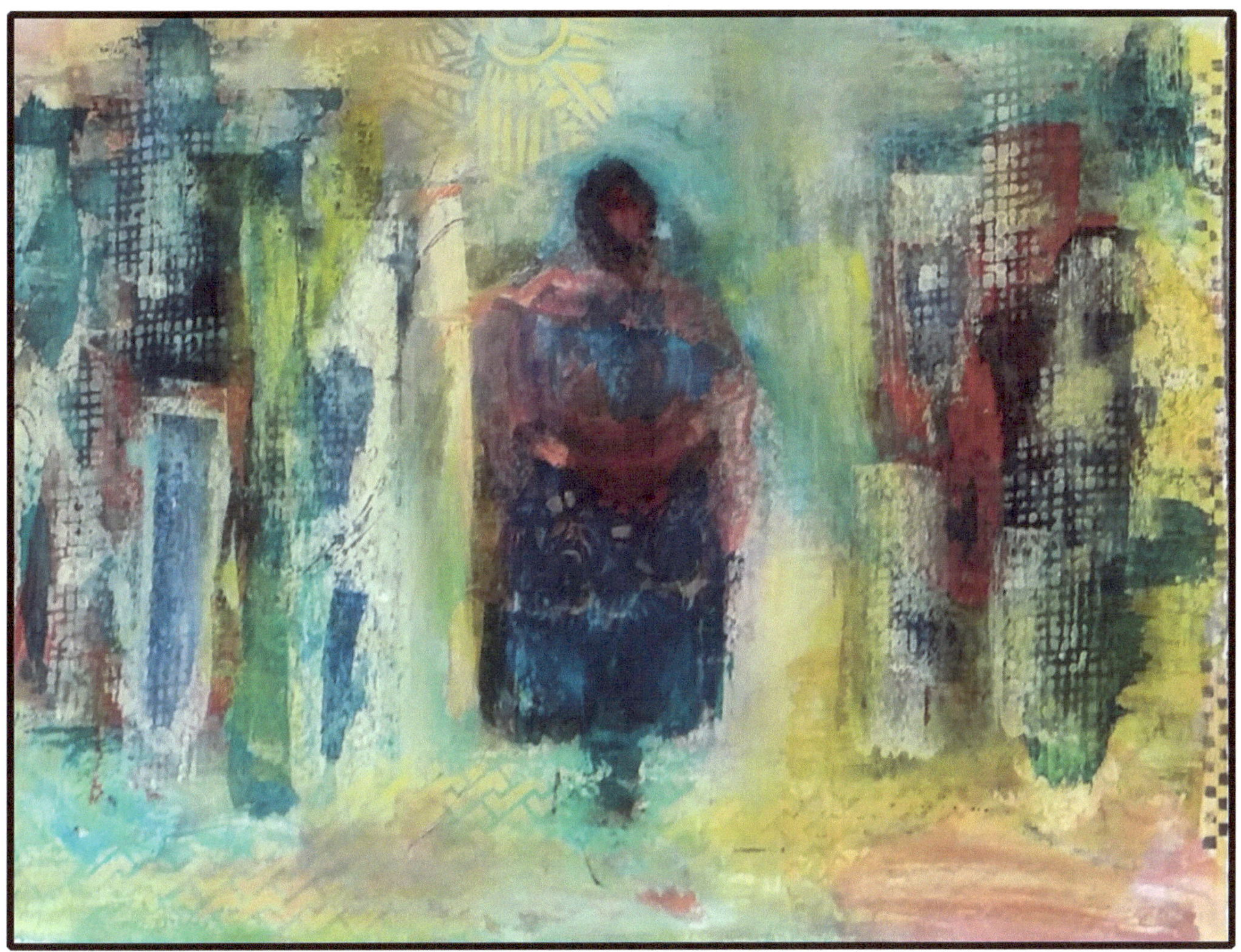

'The Immigrant'   acrylic by Victoria Kempf

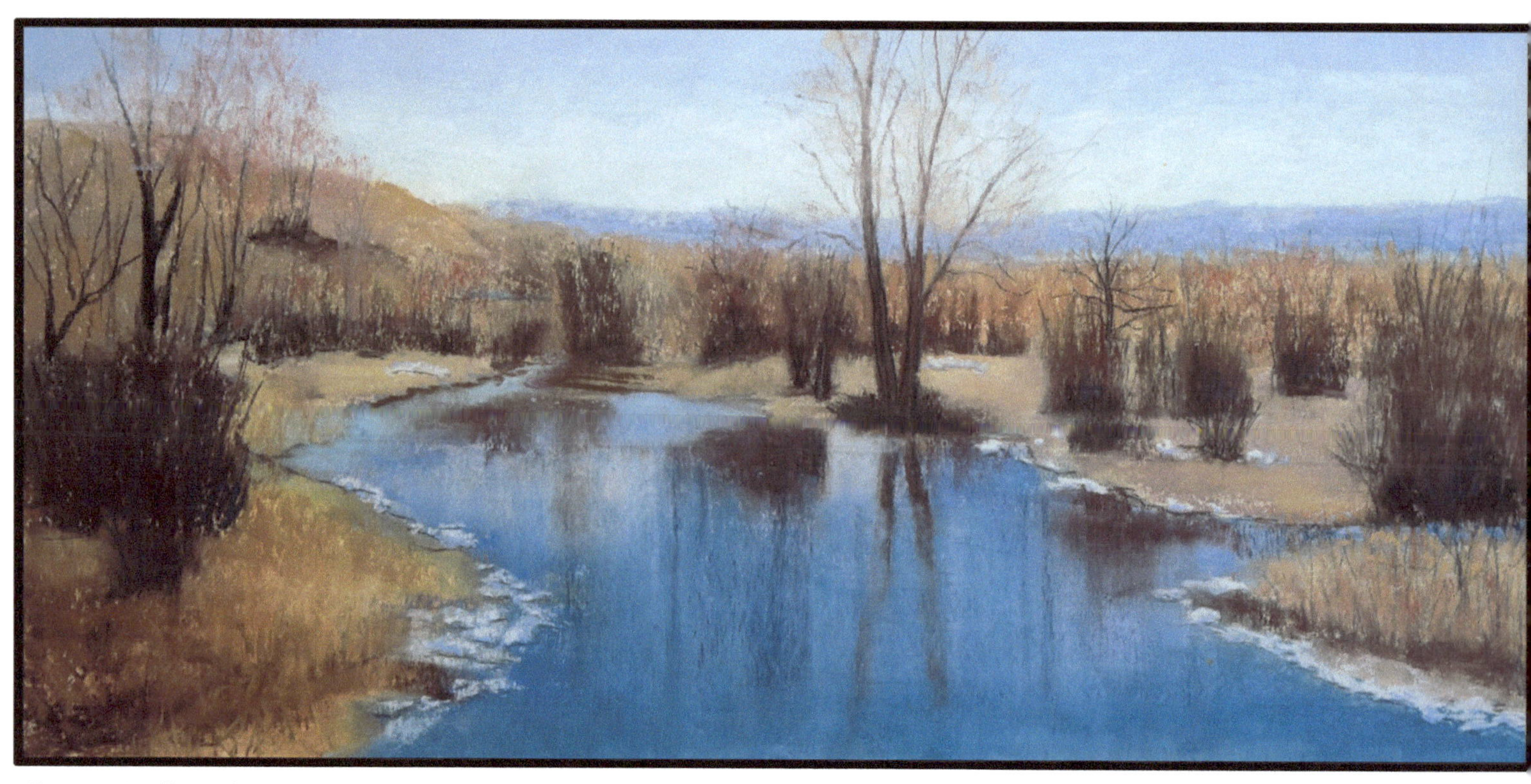

'Laramie River'   pastel by Diane Edwards

Creation

In the beginning ... the earth was unformed and void...
Genesis

On the first day I was a child playing alone in the sandbox.

On the second day I met you and the world shifted just a little.

On the third we conceived sons who were born in great waves of wonder.

On the fourth they grew tall and waved goodbye as they left for college and
the world.

And on the fifth we held grandchildren high in the air and measured their
progress in pencil on the closet door-frame.

On the sixth day we grew gray, wrote poems
        and went for walks that took forty years.

On the seventh day we rested on memories and laurels and riverbanks.

    And whatever shall we do
        next week, my dear?

Lorrie Wolfe
2nd Place Poetry

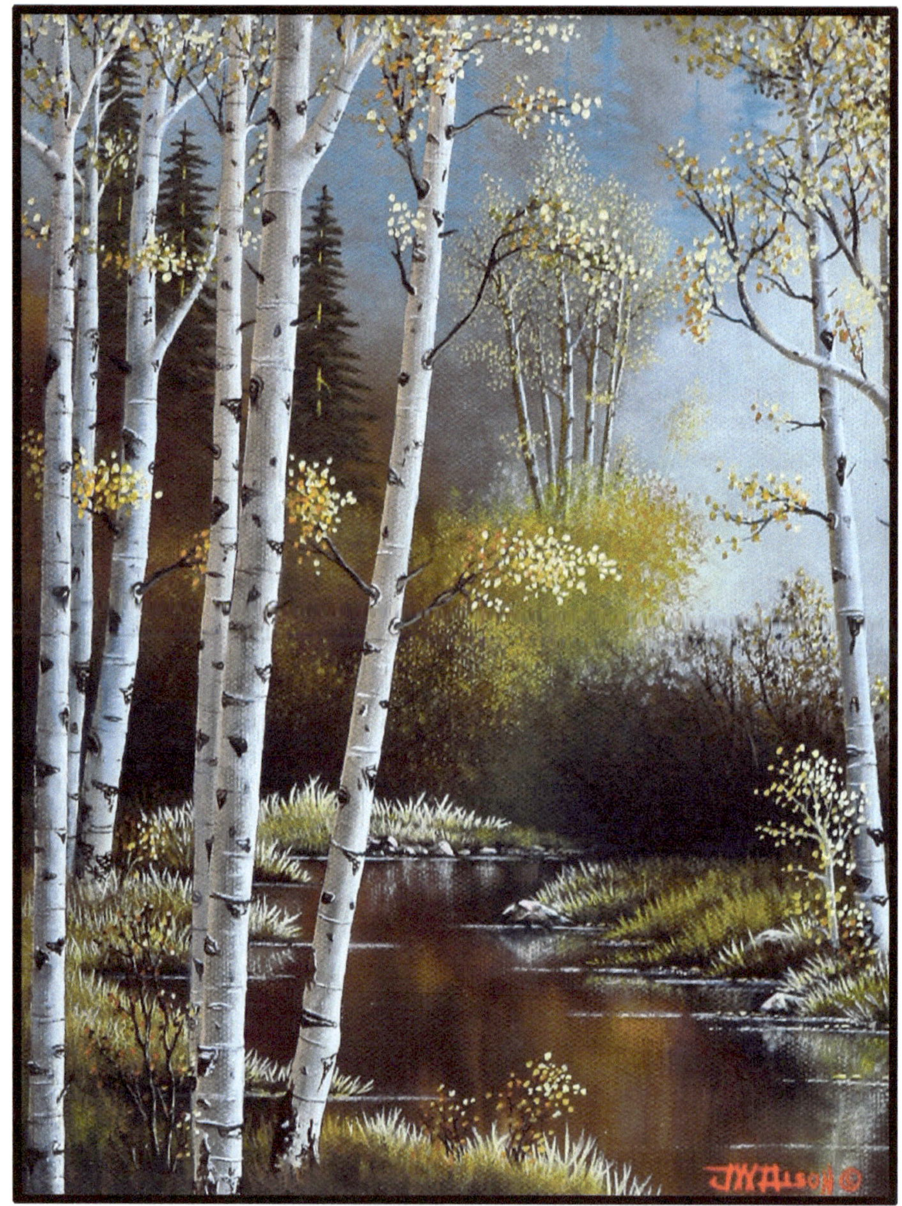

'Autumn Mist'   Oil by   Jack Olsen

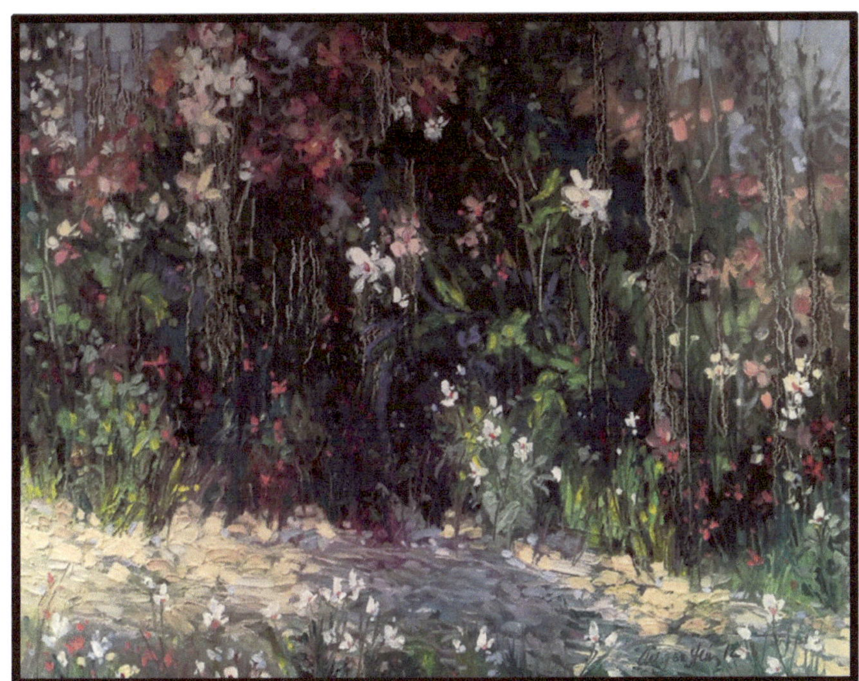

'Path in the Garden'
oil by Dan Augenstein

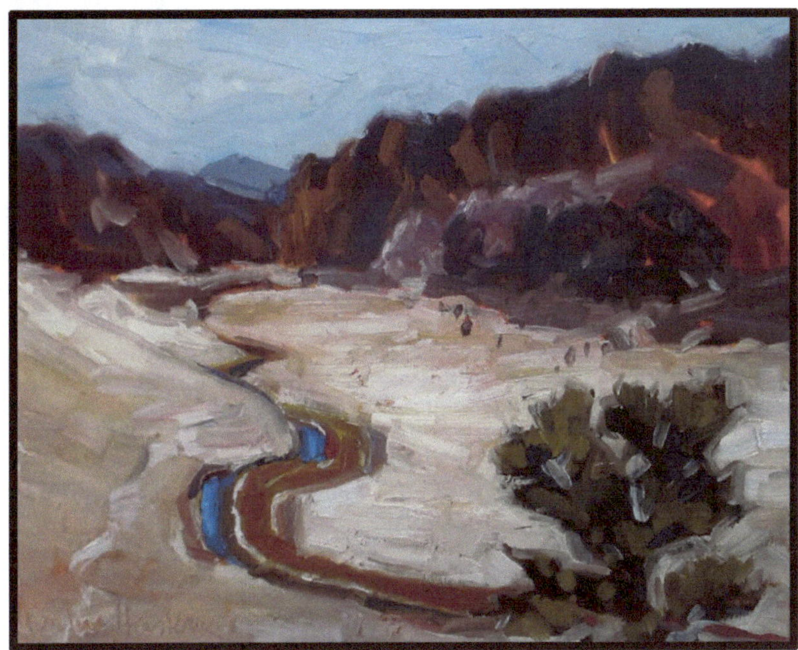

'To The Flatirons'
oil by Susan Haskins

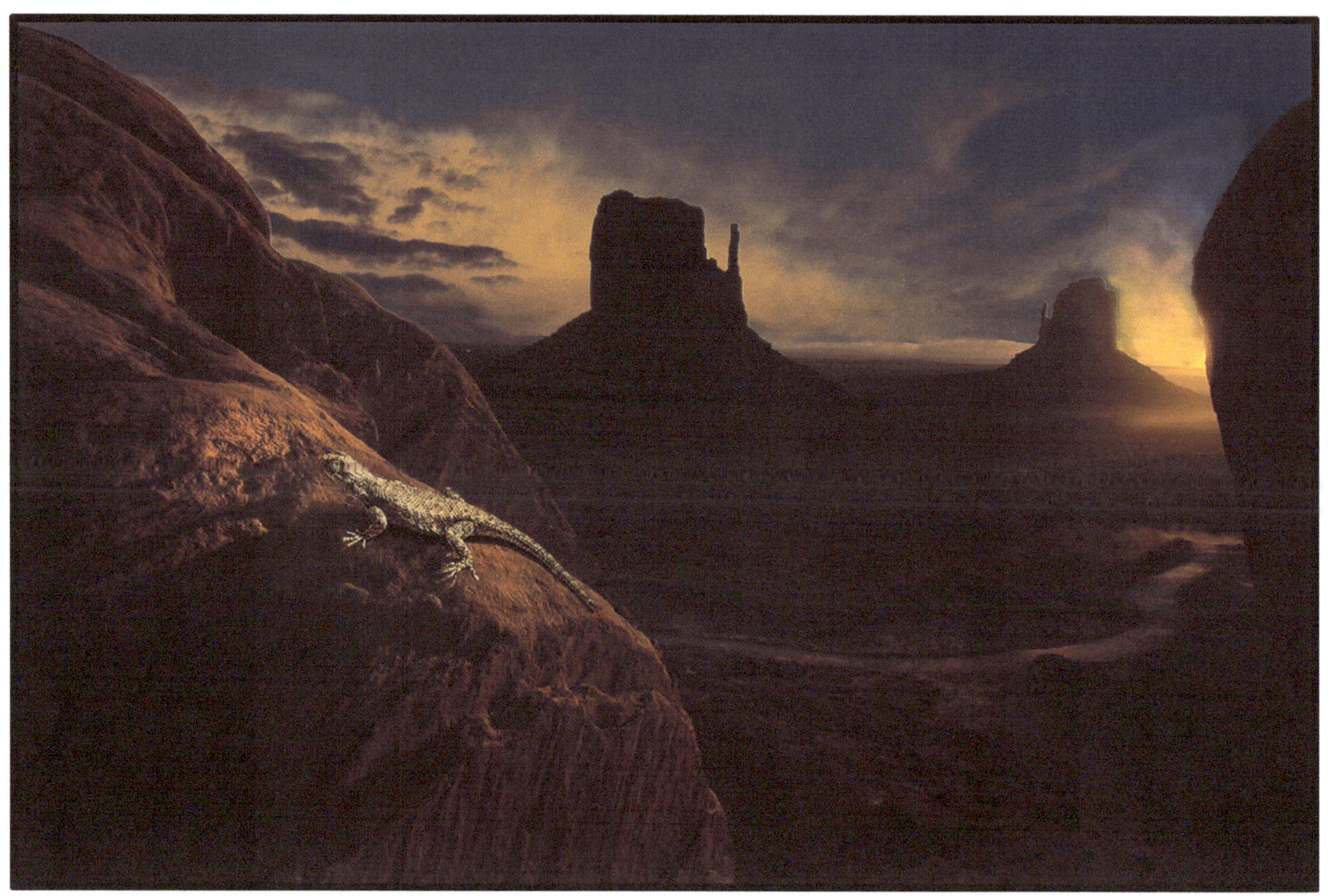

'Lizard At Sunrise'   Ruth Sprain

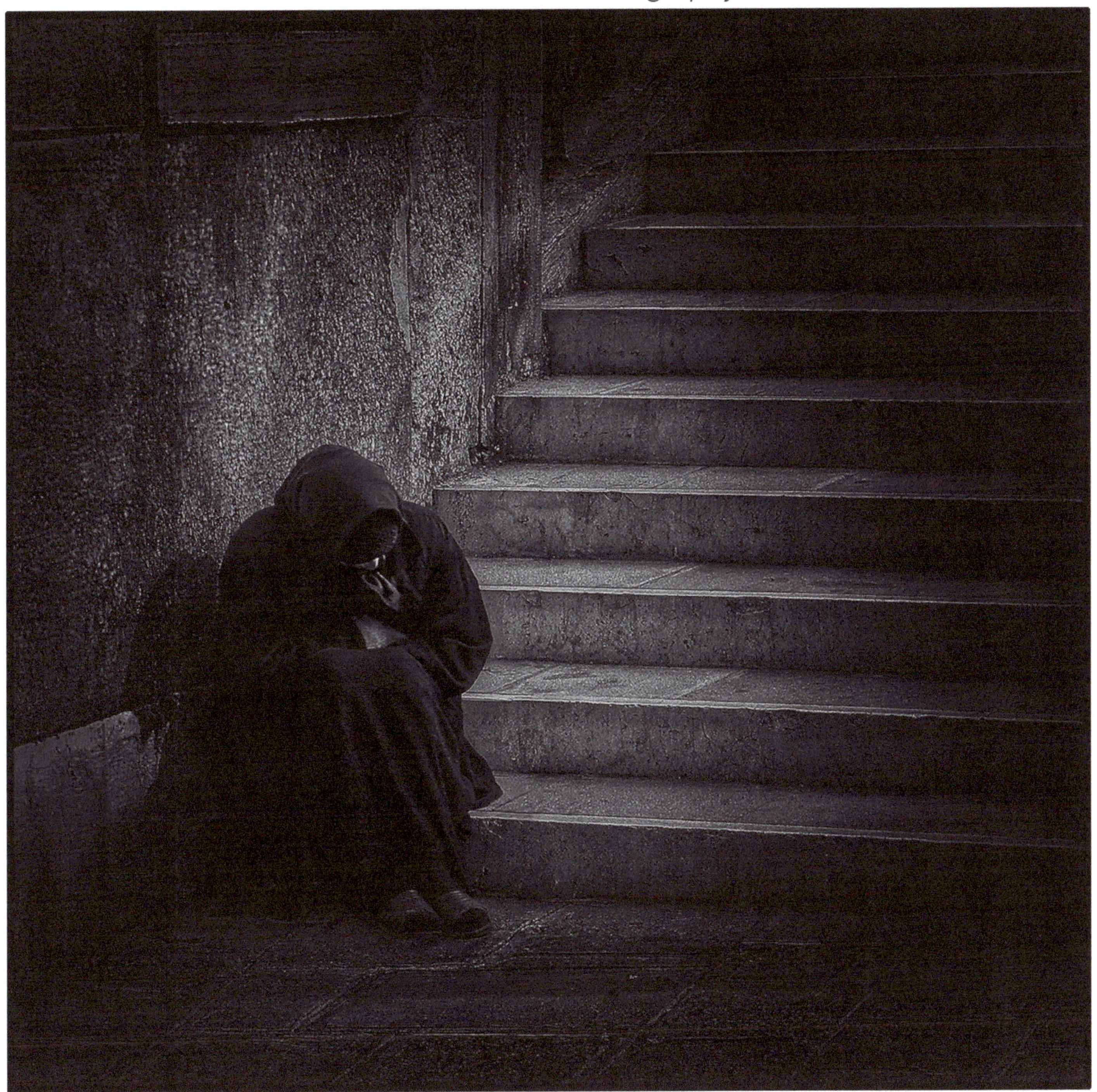

'Beggar Woman'   Gordon Middleton

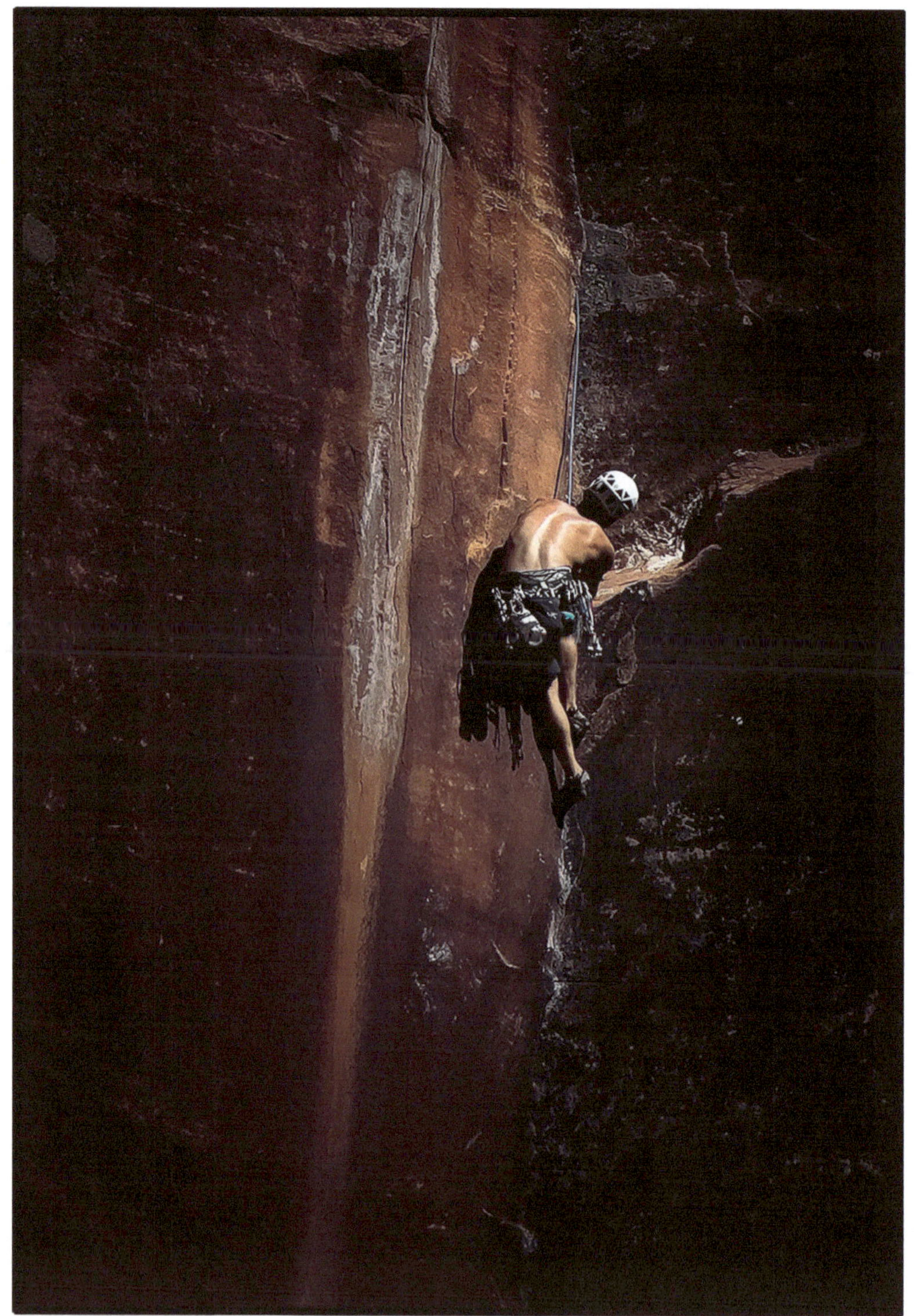

'Setting Goals'

Keith Clements

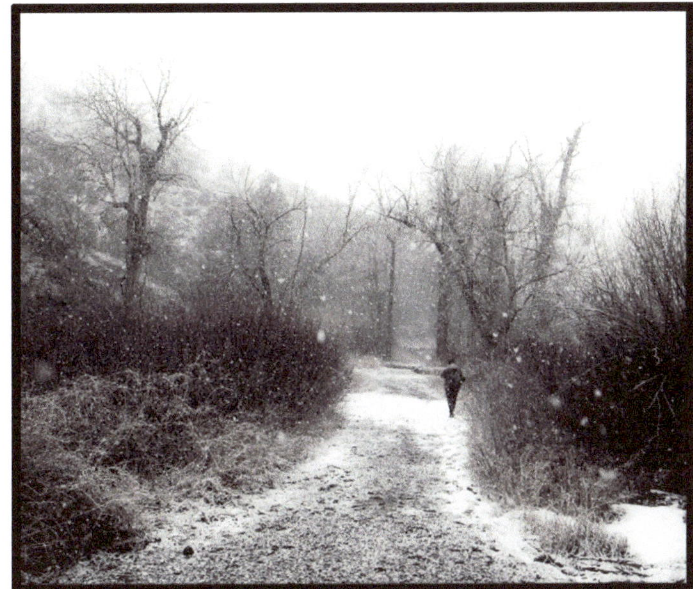

'Whos Woods These Are'   Roween Weems

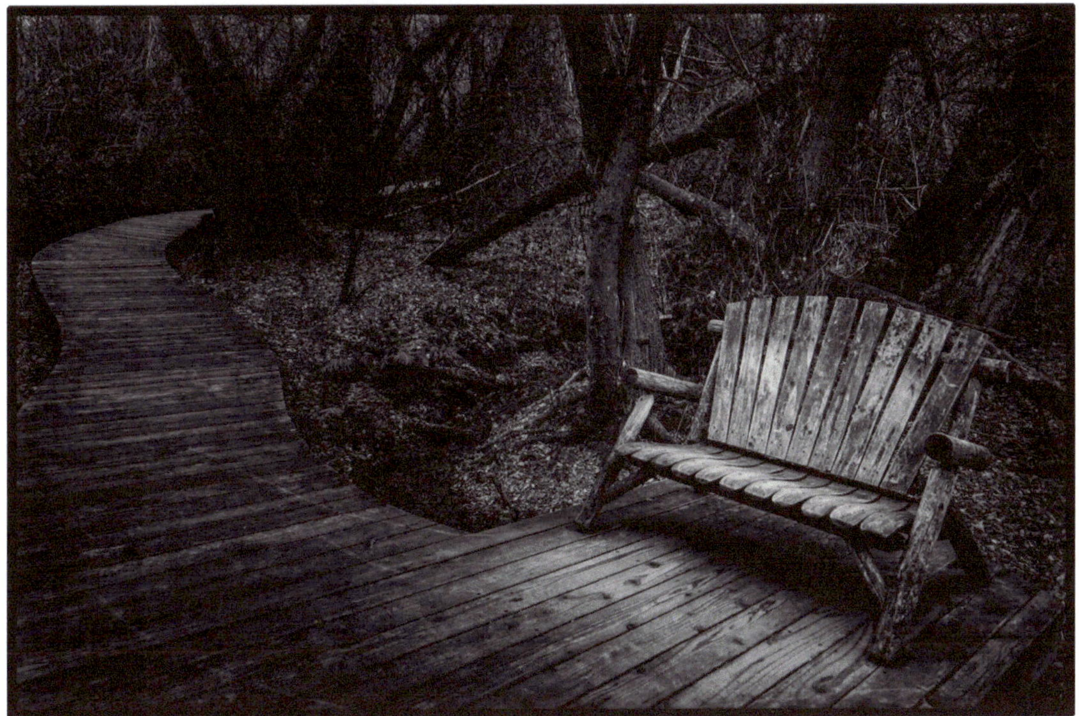

'Bench & Boardwalk'   Michael Wilcox

There are things known
and there are things unknown.
In between there are doors.

๛

~Jim Morrison

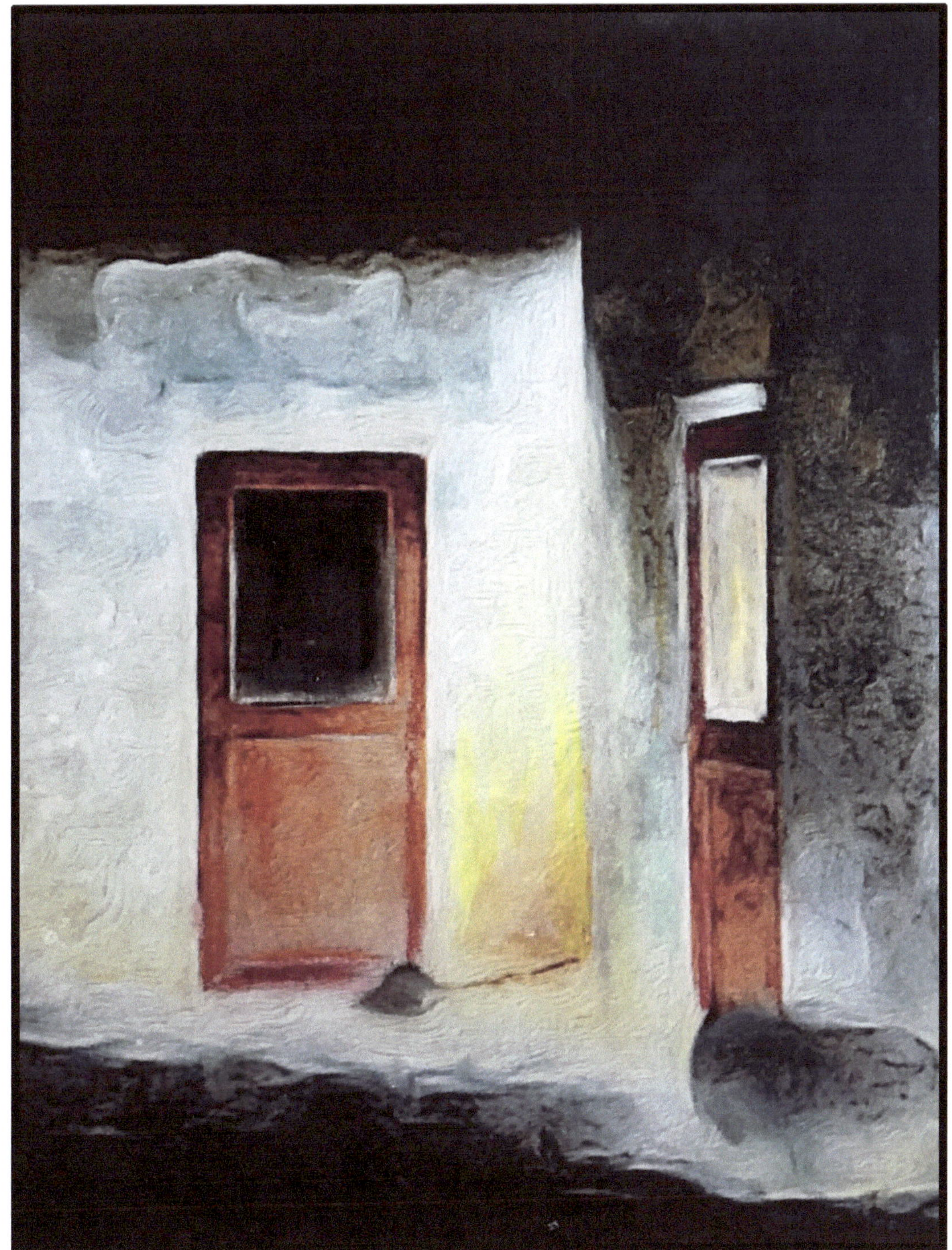

'Choices'   *Annie Surbeck*

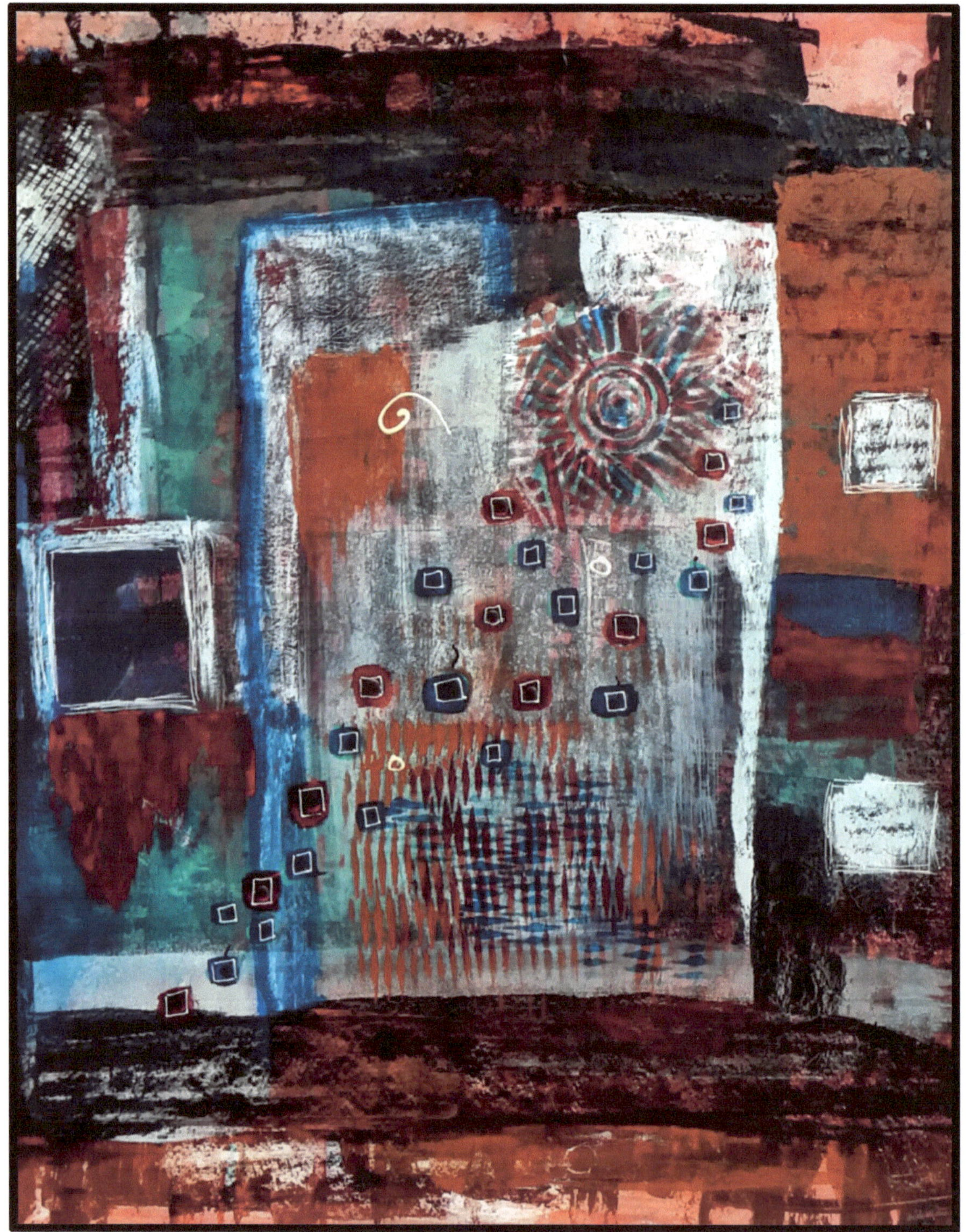

'Choose This Door'   Victoria Kempf

This Is How You Begin

You must do the thing you think you cannot do.
Eleanor Roosevelt

when what they say is
can't won't never amount to
who do you think you --

stand, pick up your wounded pen
they can't pay you enough
to make you stop

you lose track of time
you would do this anyway
this thing you can't *not* do

it has a life all its own
it thrums
wakes you in the night

there's a ring
the Operator speaks
it's always collect

you take the call

Lorrie Wolfe
Honorable Mention/Poetry

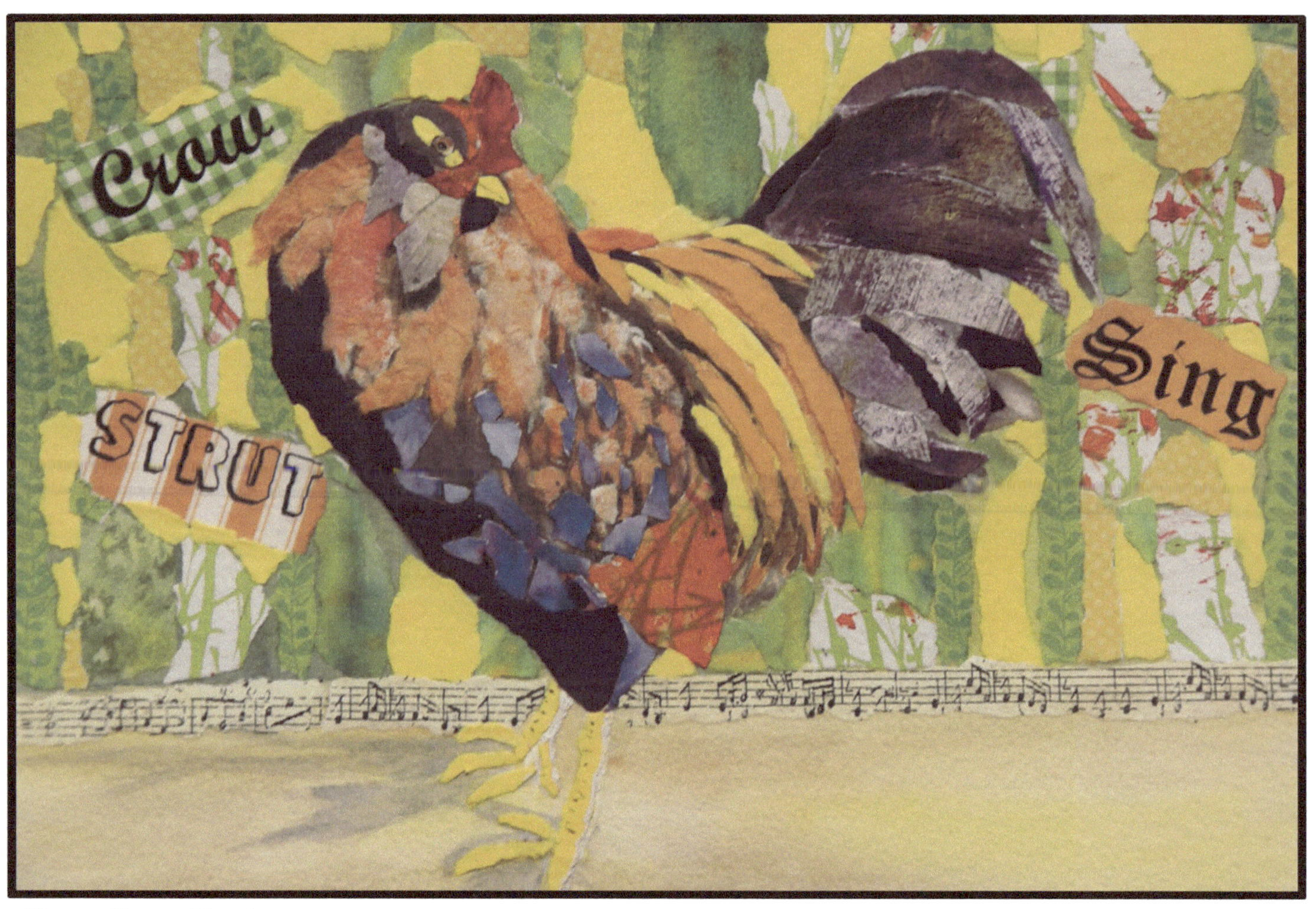

'Strut, Crow, Sing'

Vickie McCargar

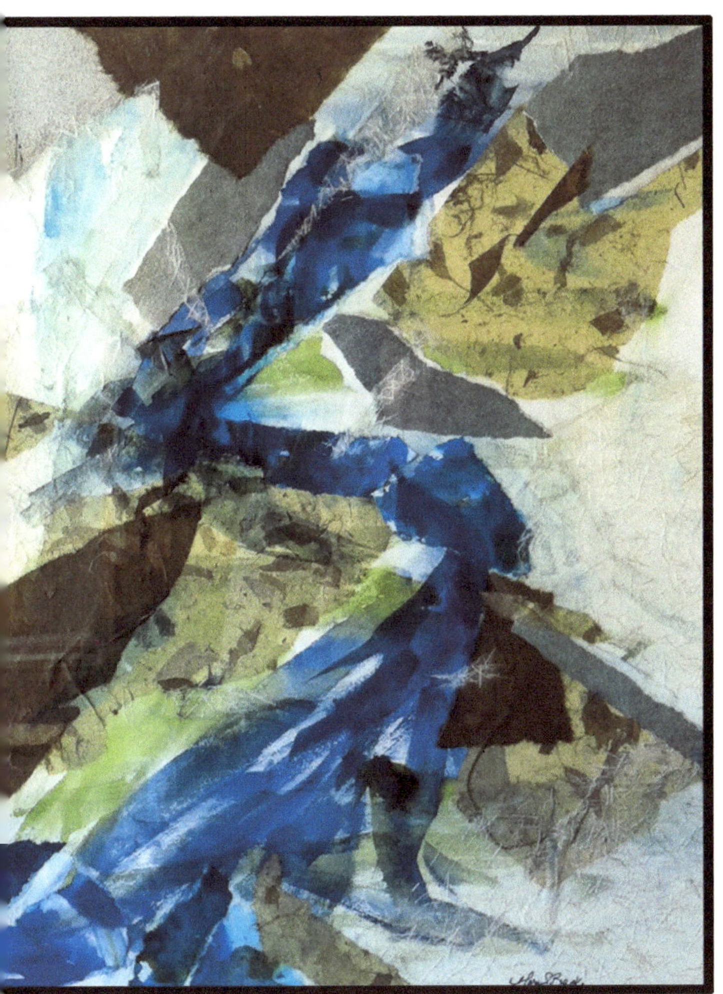

'River Run'   Mary Benke

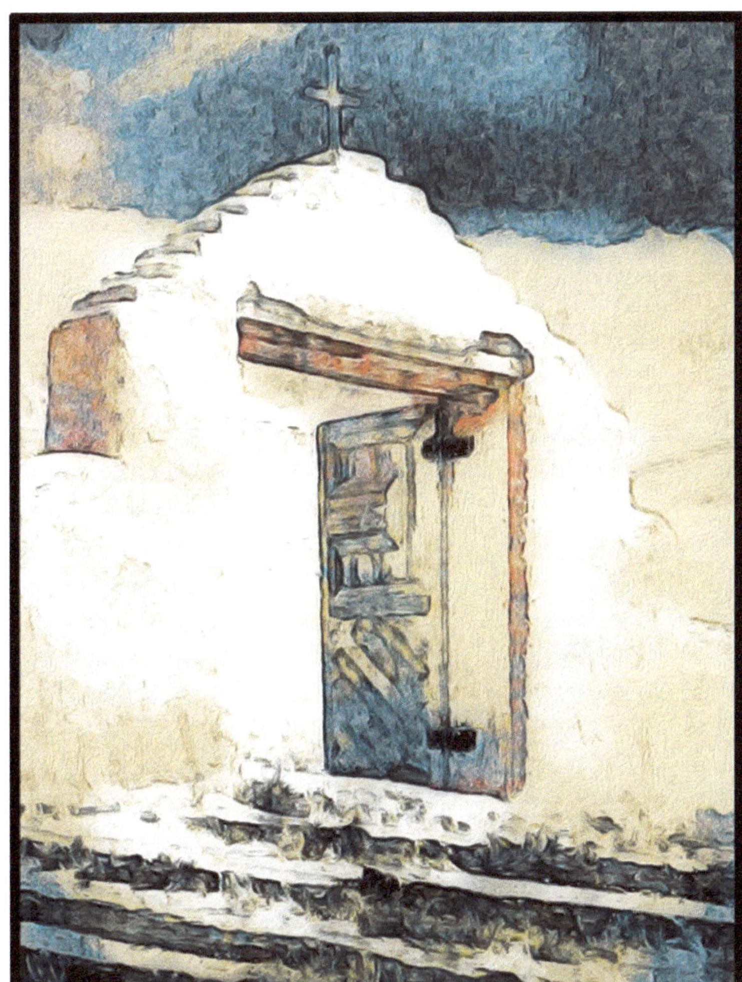

'Redemption'   Annie Surbeck

The Gate and The Door

The gate creaks open,
Humble sound of regret threading
A quiet course to my straining ears
Amid the other, more strident voices
Of the night: the wind wraps long,
Brittle fingers around the house to keep
The intruder out, crickets and junebugs
Cast their discordant songs into the darkness,
And some lone, vigilant bird sleepily sounds
A shrill alarm: but still I can hear him.
That silent, waiting figure who listens too
And catches from within my walls the echo
Of his own watchful breathing – night
Becomes midnight becomes dawn,
Hinges swing shut with a mournful groan,
And even at noon I am still straining,
Listening to his footsteps as they recede to farewell.

Cassondra Windwalker
Honorable Mention/Poetry

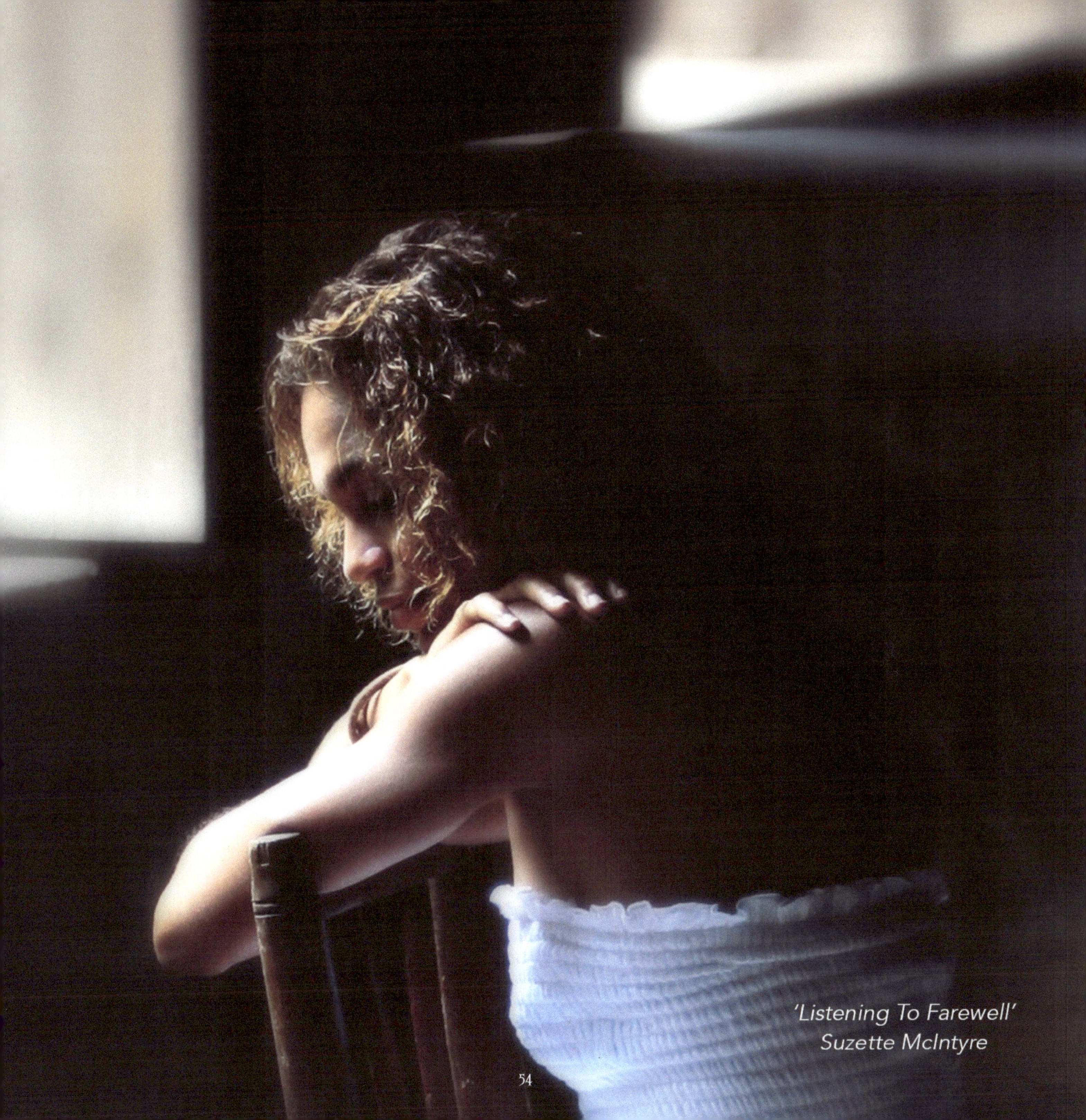

'Listening To Farewell'
Suzette McIntyre

EmPath

Change is coming.
I see it in your eyes.
I hear angels prophesy
during early morning meditation.
I see a crabapple tree blossoming
its mass of roots reaching deep,
hiding a symbol in its tangles in dark soil.

Uncover the stone prepared for you,
shaped like a key,
its small specks could be read like tea leaves.
Hang it around your neck.
Meander toward the garden of garlic,
smell juniper and peppermint growing
beside the weathered picket fence.

Notice the red pepper ristra
hung by the entryway to ward off evil.
watch the clouds and their unique shapes
forming just above the iron gate.
Are they guides for you…
your spirit animal leading you
as you merge onto this new path?

Breathe, lean into your body.
Look around, listen, feel the mystery.
The signs, the light.
Yes, you are ready.
Give simple warning to those who need to know.
Bravely open the garden gate latch,
set out into your future.

Lori Nunnally
Honorable Mention/Poetry

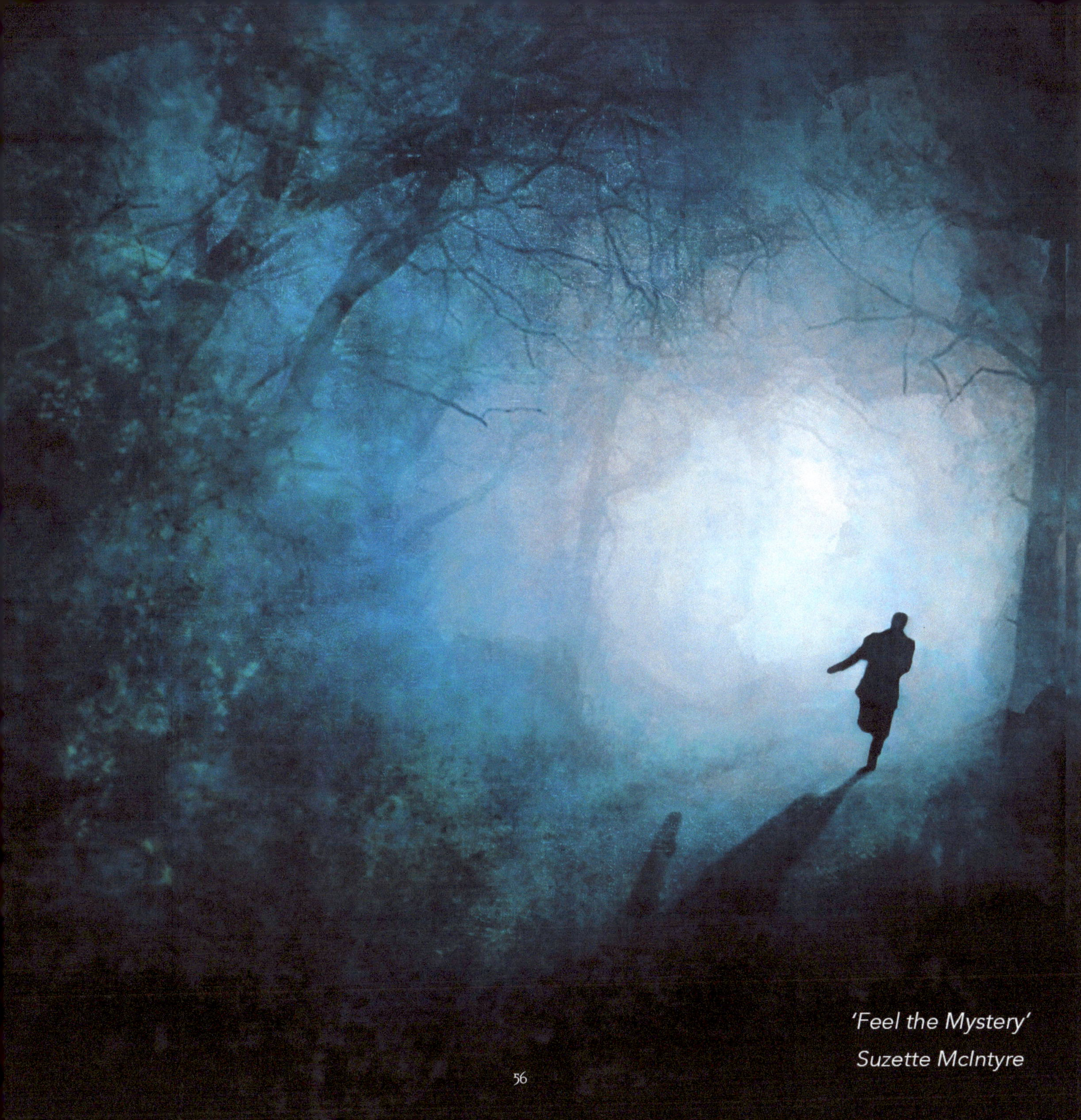

'Feel the Mystery'
Suzette McIntyre

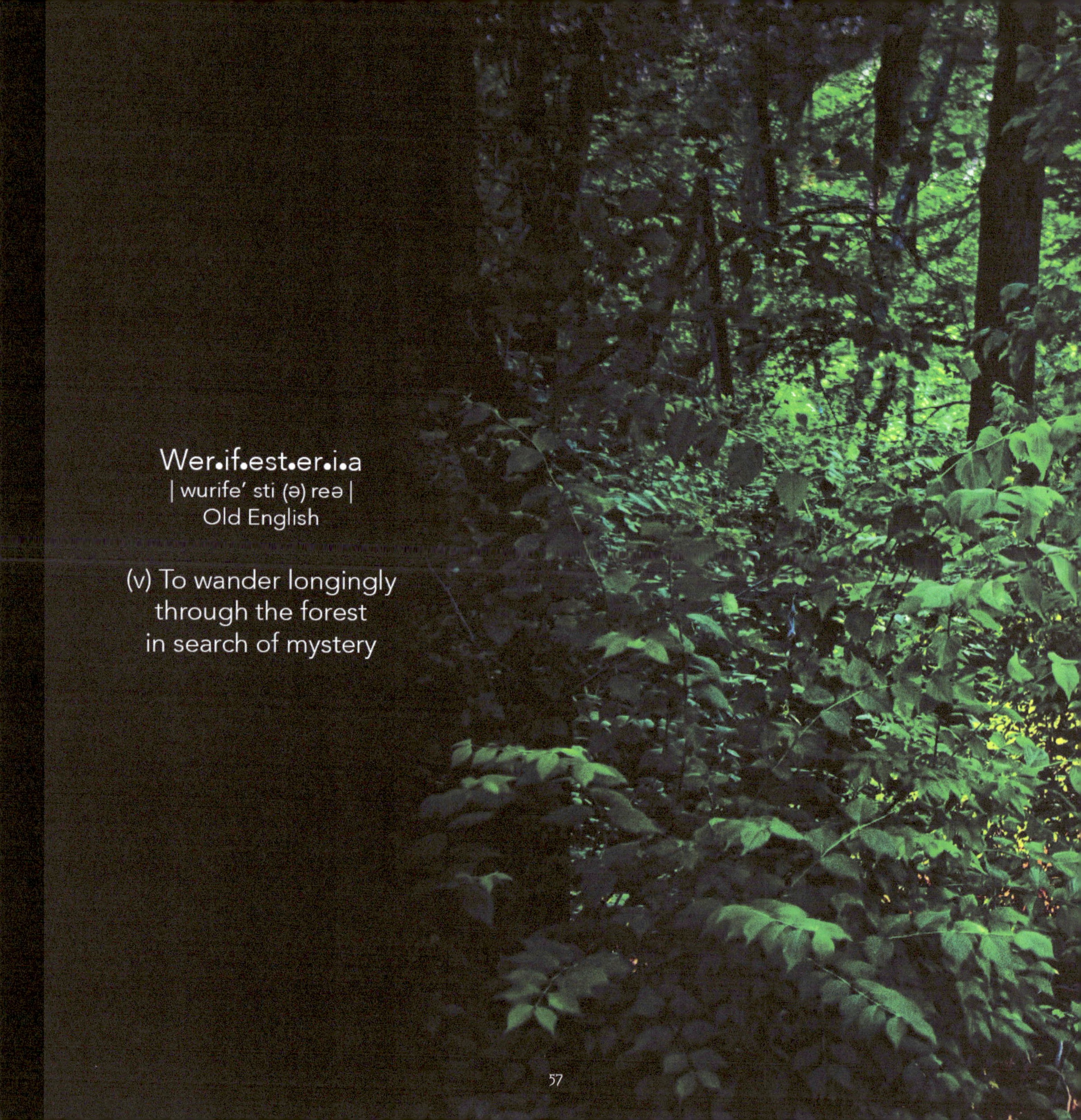

Wer·if·est·er·i·a
| wurifeʹ sti (ə) reə |
Old English

(v) To wander longingly
through the forest
in search of mystery

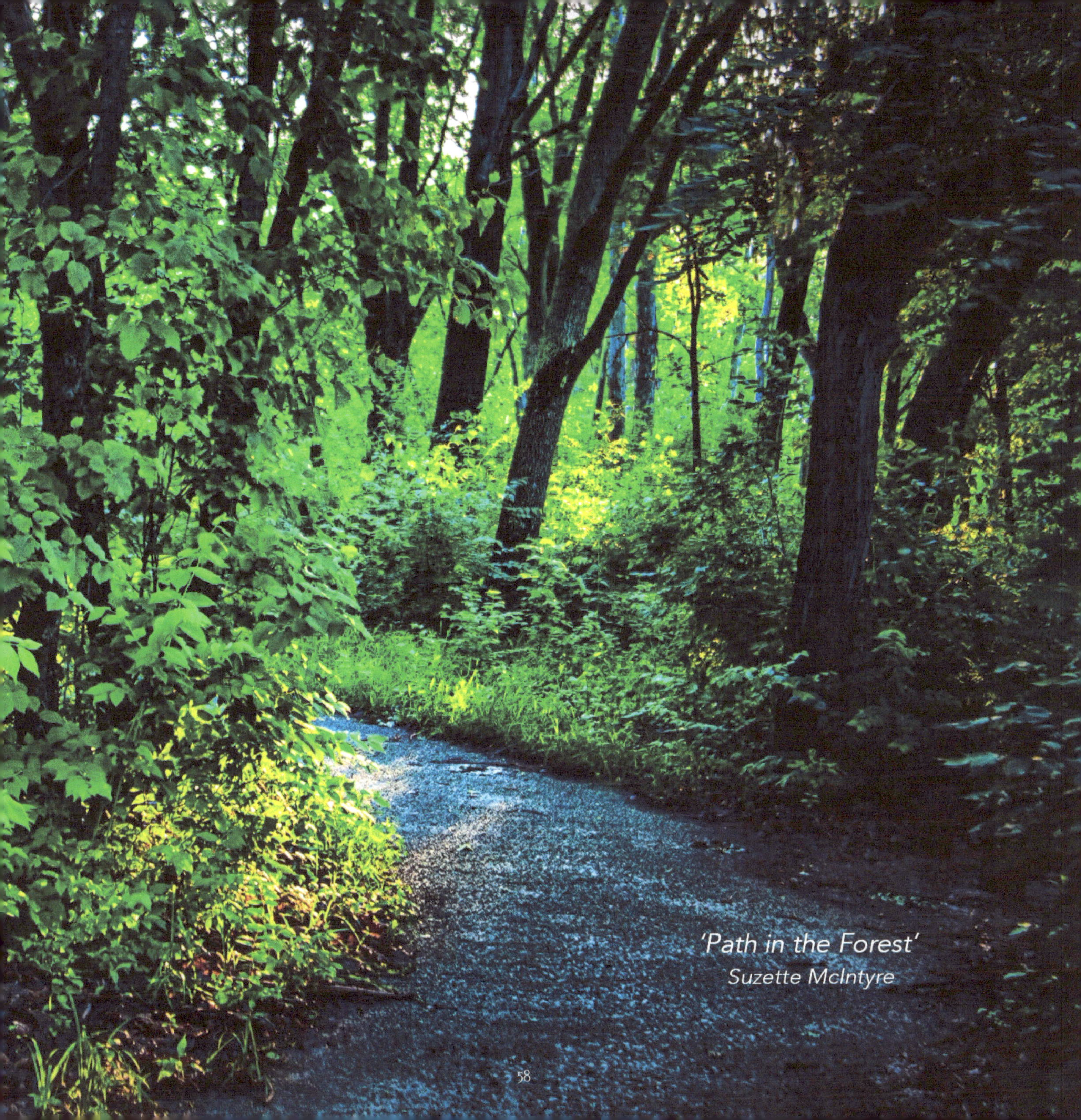

'Path in the Forest'
Suzette McIntyre

Freedom

Rows of names
Taps rises from a monument
Respect for lives lost
Humbled by their sacrifice
As immense gratitude takes hold.

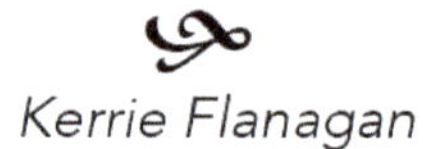

Kerrie Flanagan

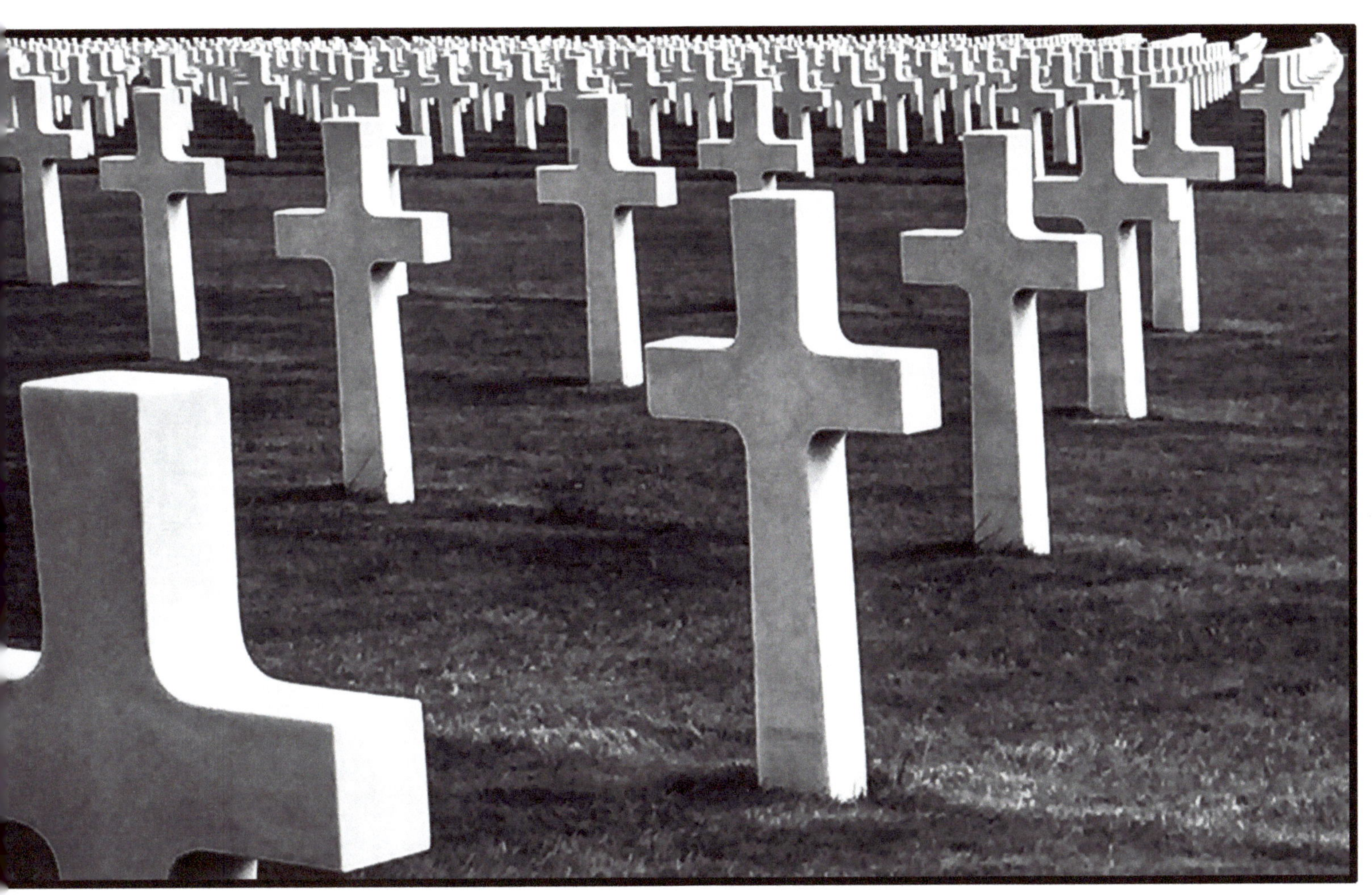

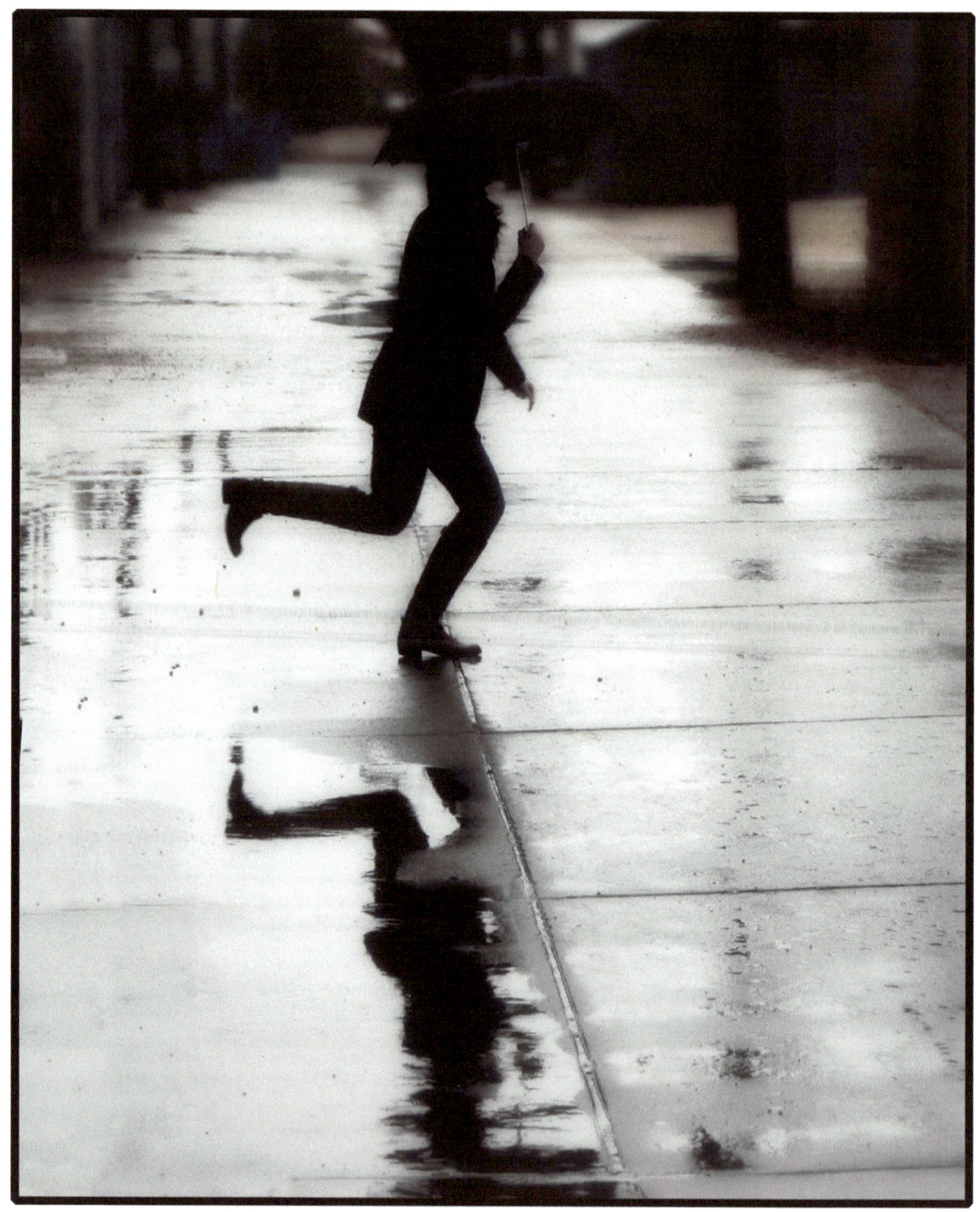

Finding Joy

Happiness, bliss
Jumping, splashing, laughing
Singing in the
Rain

❧

Kerrie Flanagan

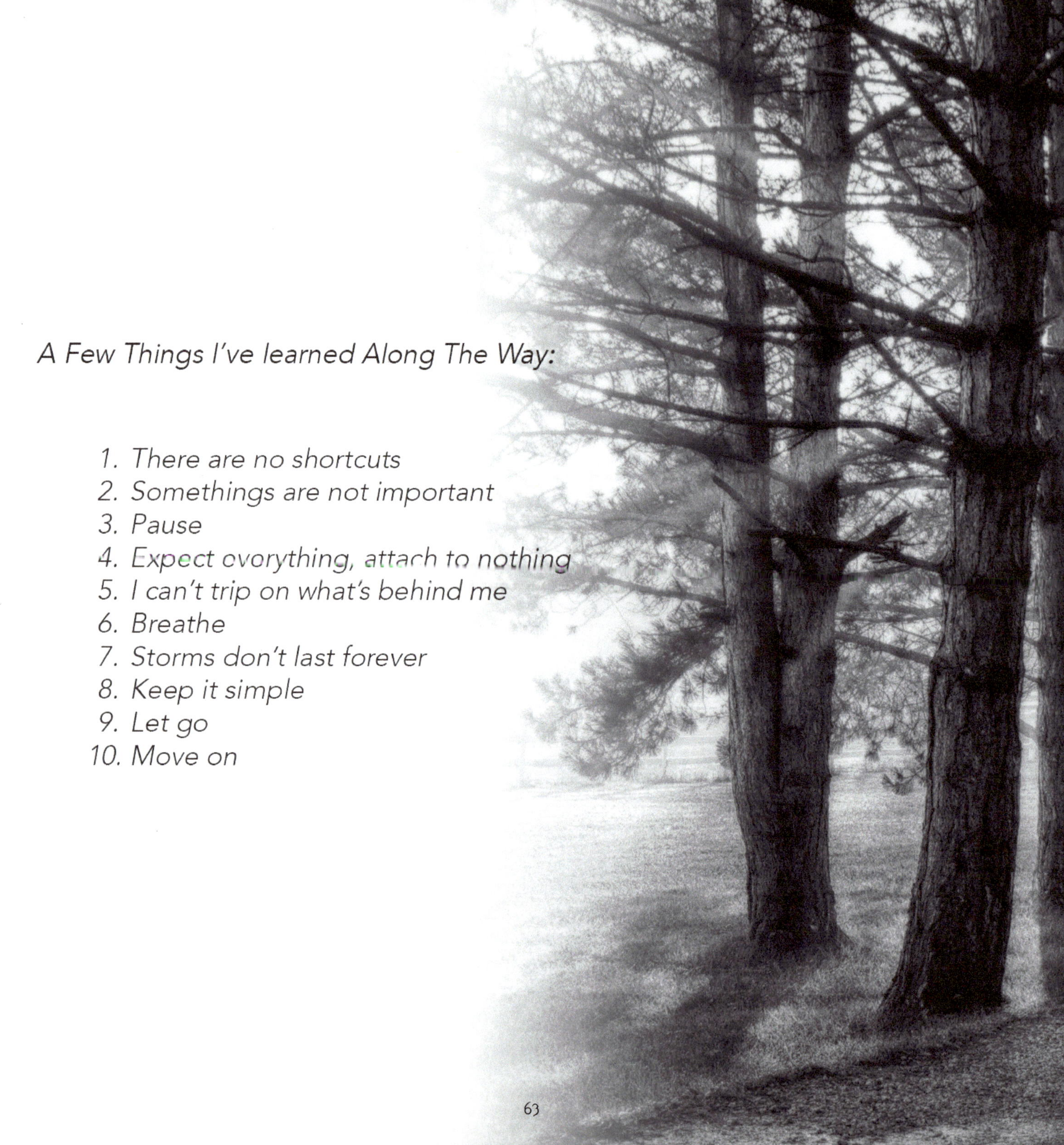

A Few Things I've learned Along The Way:

1. *There are no shortcuts*
2. *Somethings are not important*
3. *Pause*
4. *Expect everything, attach to nothing*
5. *I can't trip on what's behind me*
6. *Breathe*
7. *Storms don't last forever*
8. *Keep it simple*
9. *Let go*
10. *Move on*

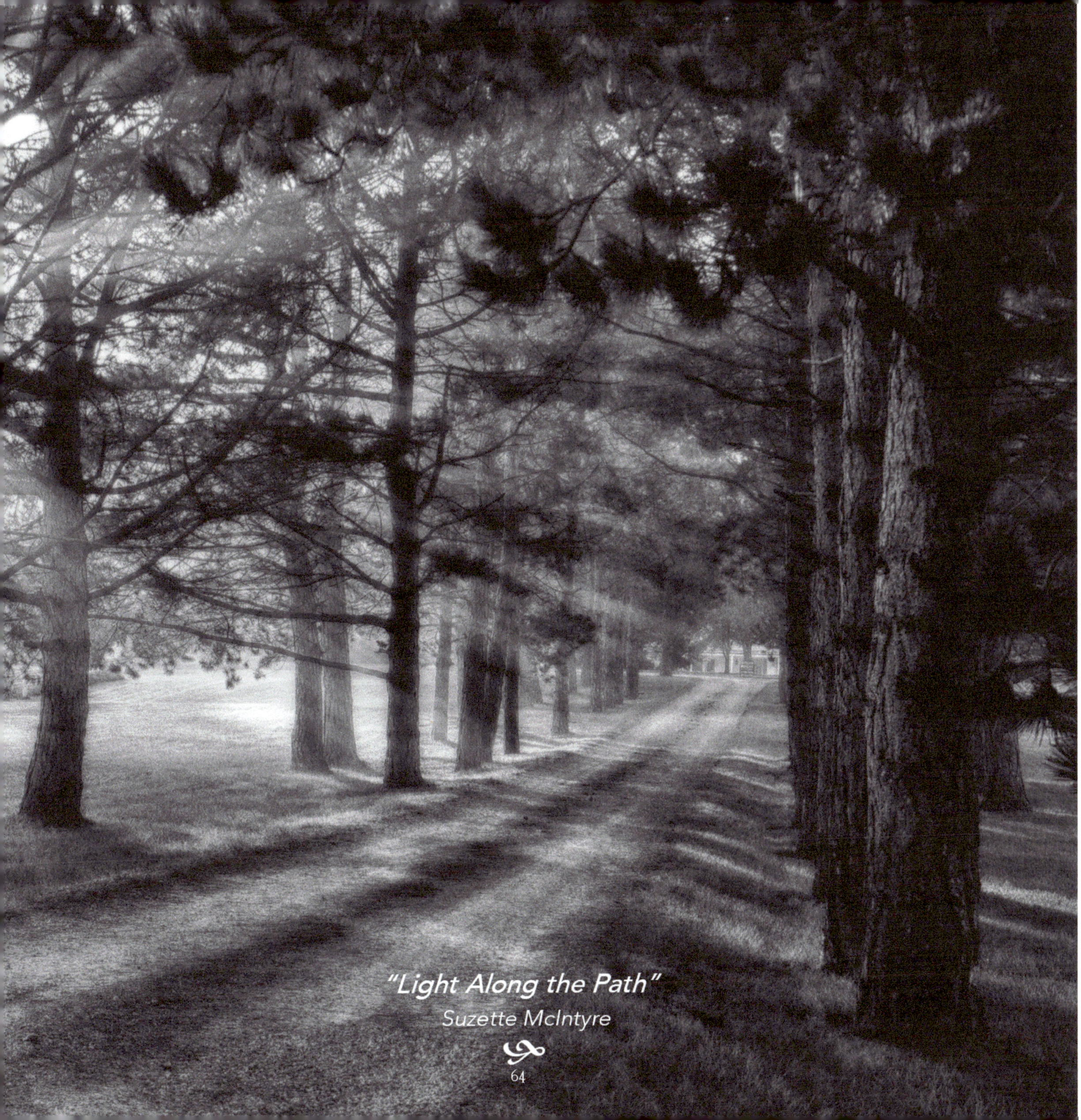

"Light Along the Path"
Suzette McIntyre

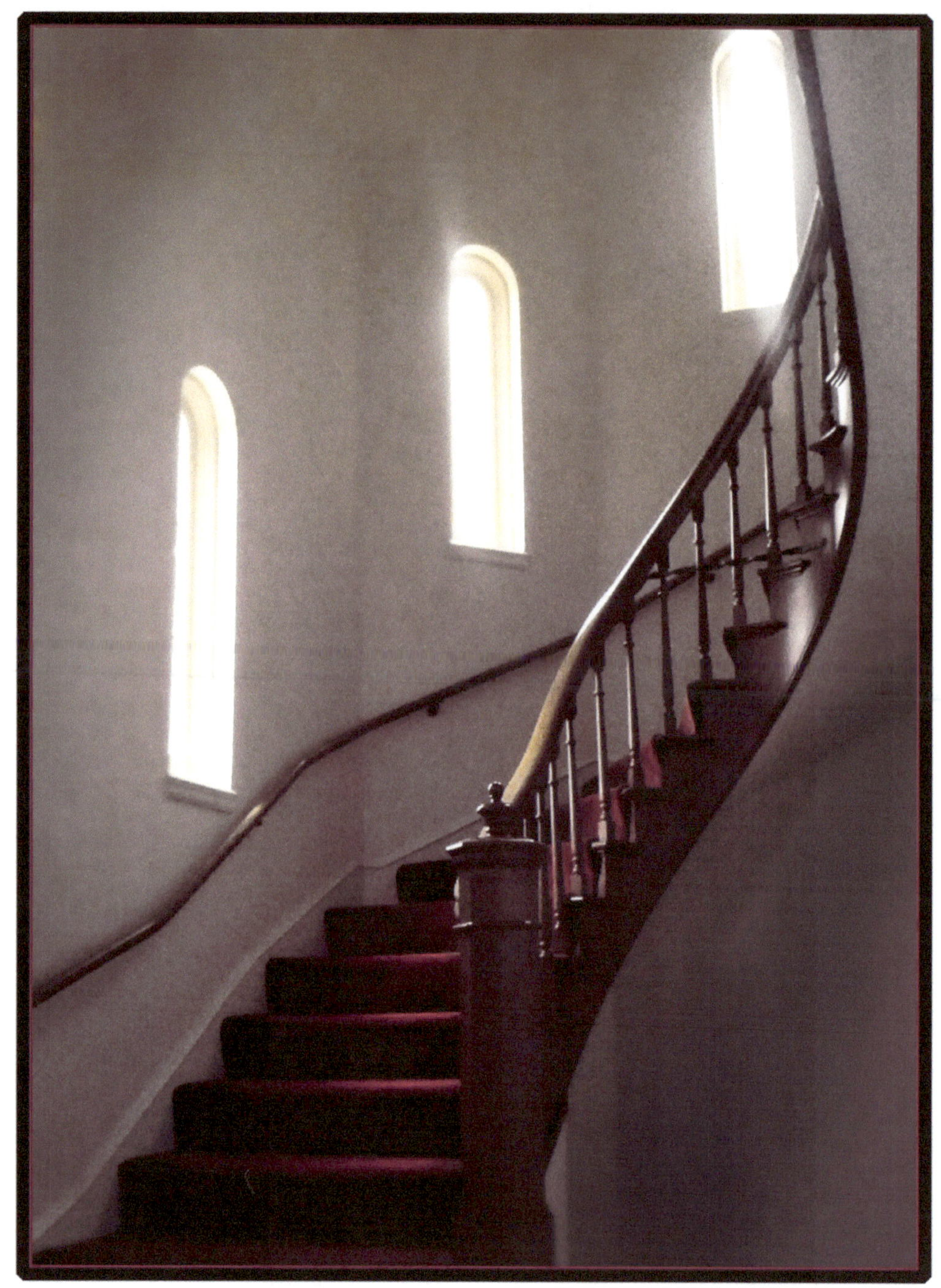

Enlightenment

Deep breaths
Quiet your mind
Go far into yourself
Seek the love and light from above
Fulfilled

ও

Kerrie Flanagan

Anonymous

Tourists walking by
Some notice, others do not
No one asks his name

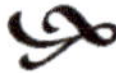

Kerrie Flanagan

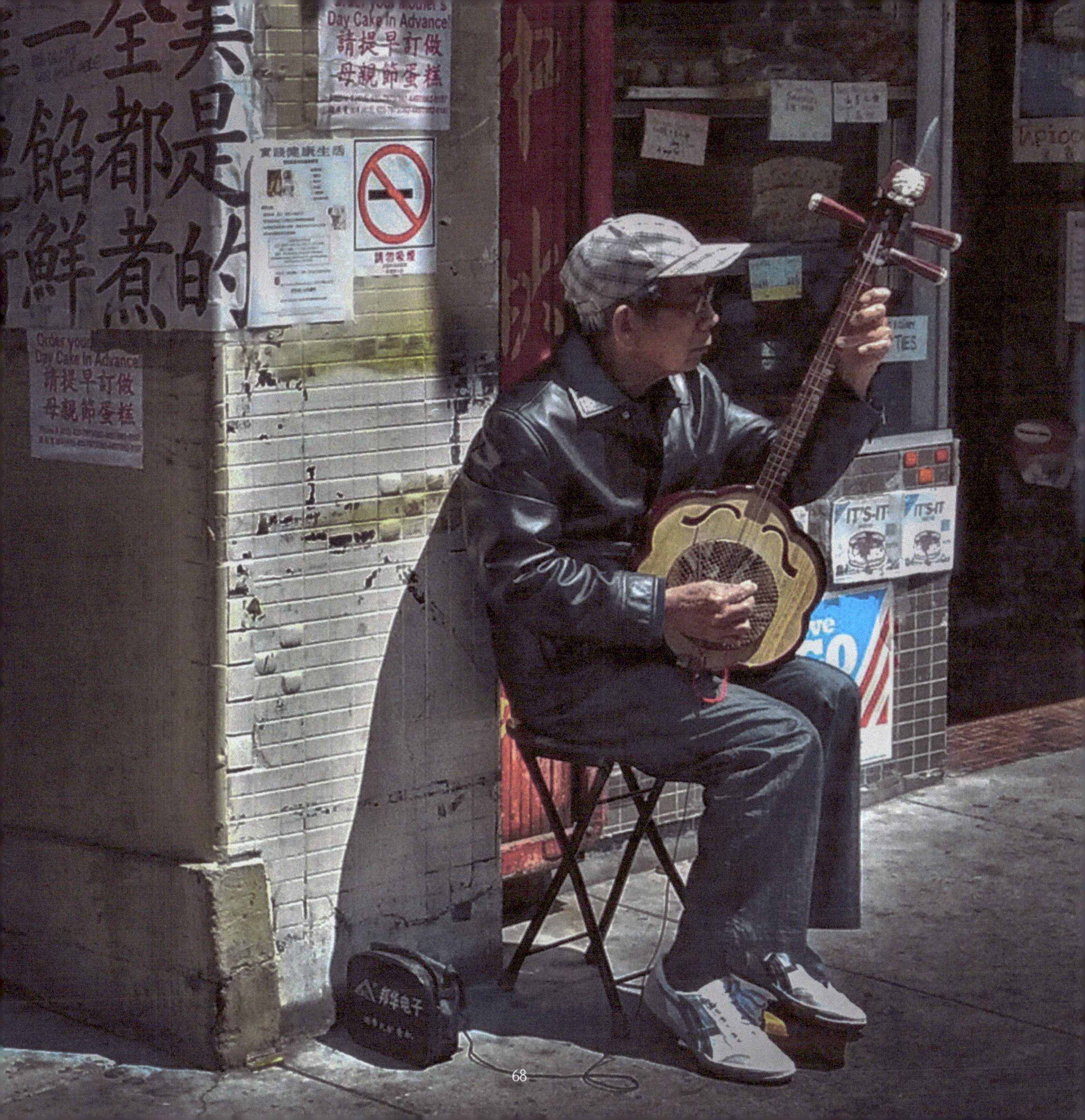

請提早訂做
母親節蛋糕
Order your Mother's
Day Cake In Advance!
一全美
餡都是
鮮煮的
旦是
的
實踐健康生活
Order your
Day Cake In Advance!
請提早訂做
母親節蛋糕
IT'S-IT
IT'S-IT
apioc
TIES

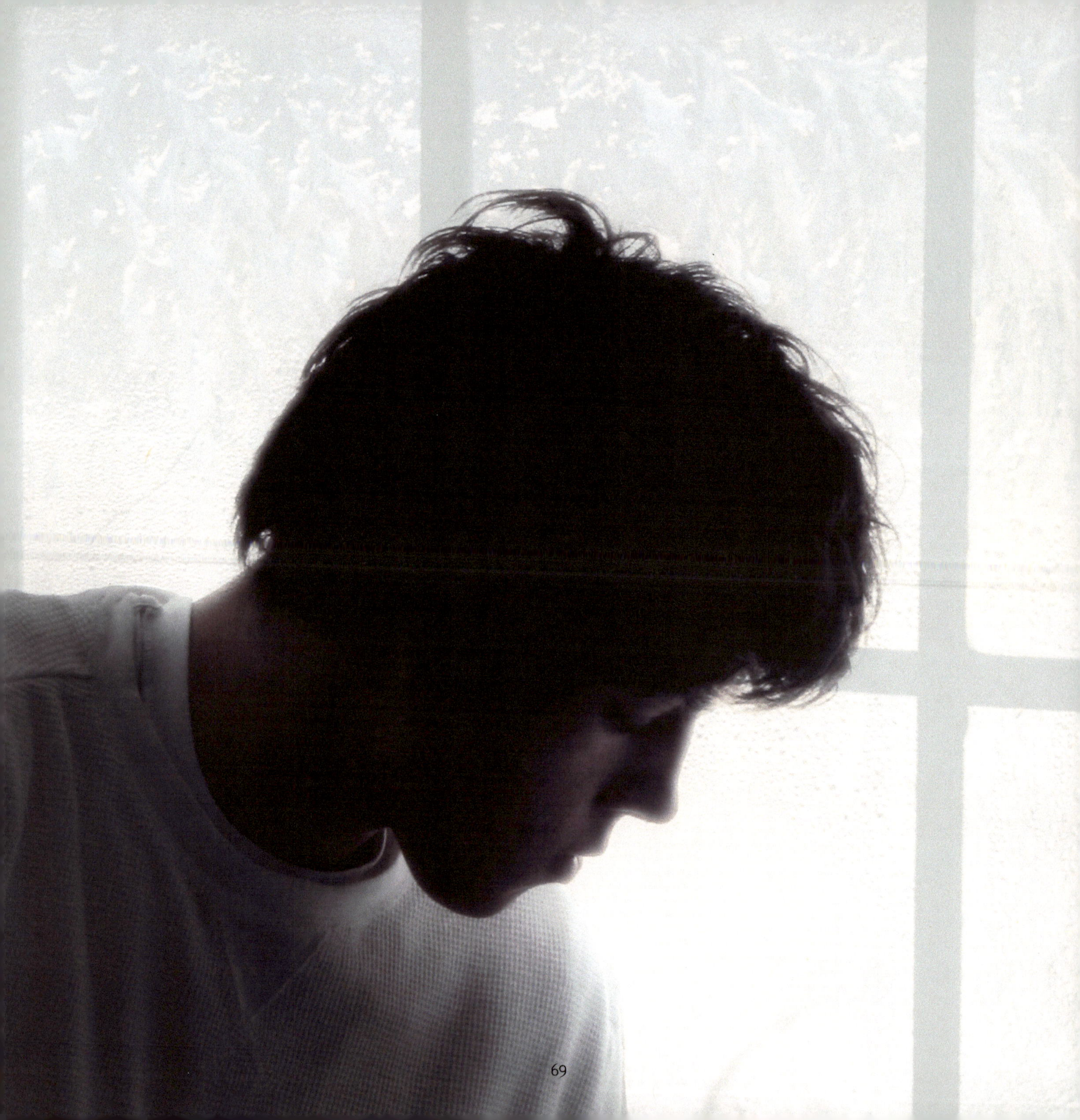

I want to photograph you in this moment,
the light softly brushing your face.

Tomorrow
it will be a memory
of a path I did not take.

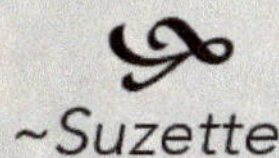

~Suzette

DON'T SETTLE

Whatever path you take,
make it one of choice
not compliance.

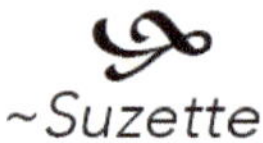

~Suzette

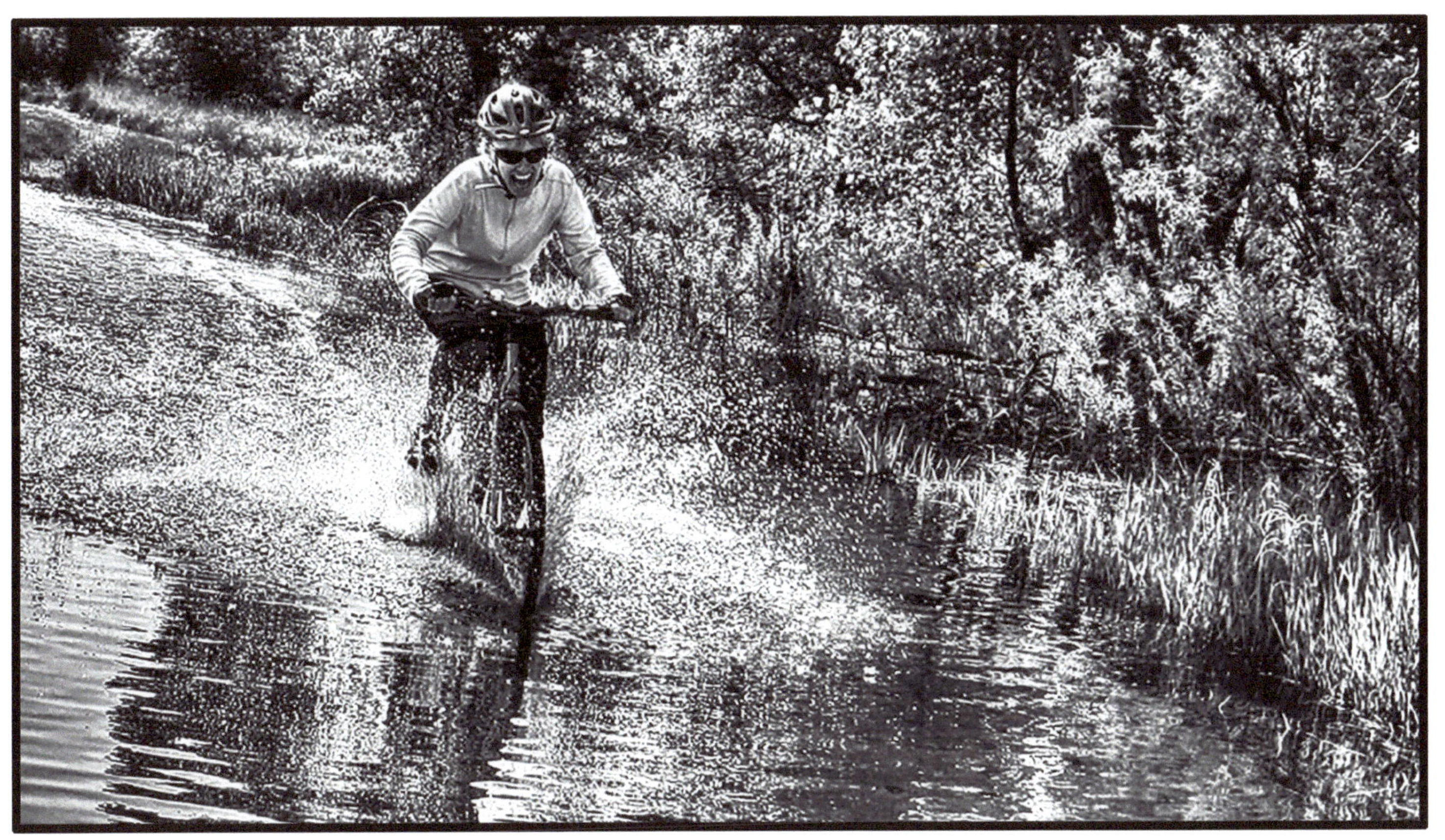

'Enjoy the Ride'

Suzette McIntyre

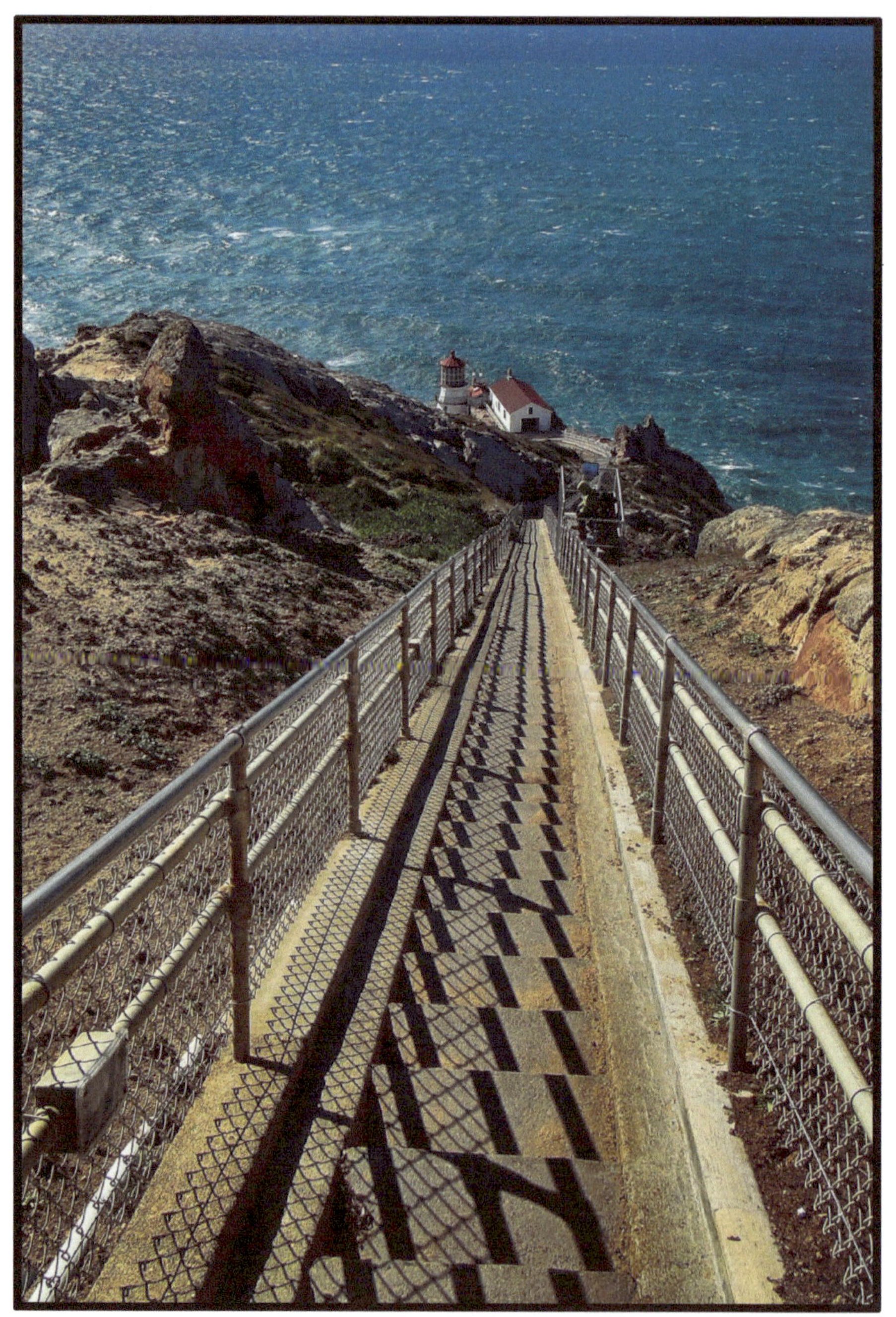

Making Memories

Two friends
One adventure
Three hundred steps to go
Wind whipping, waves crashing below
They're ready!

Kerrie Flanagan

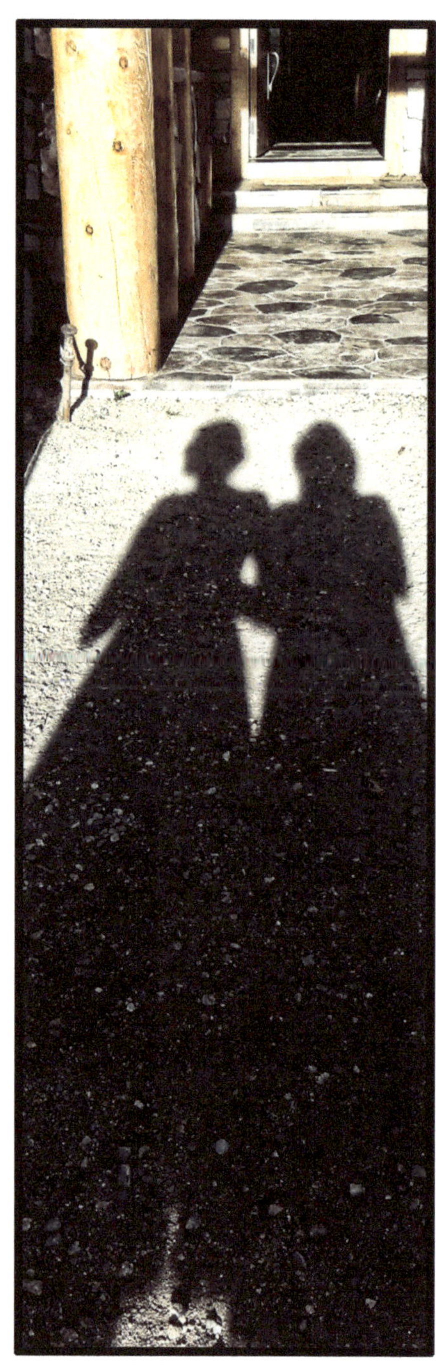

Make time to connect
with those
who mean
the most to you.

৵

Kerrie Flanagan

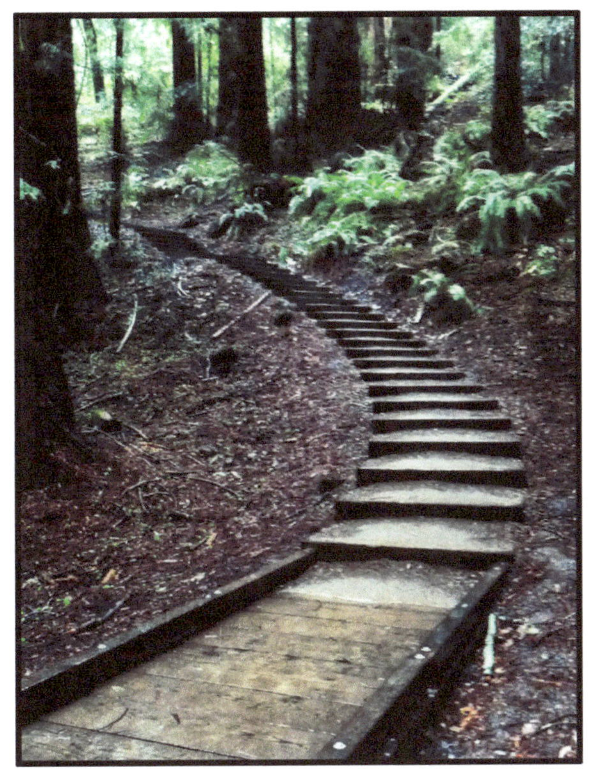

Connecting with Nature

Dampness fills the air
The quietness presses in
Calming my spirit

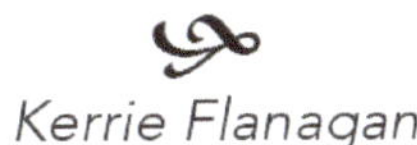

Kerrie Flanagan

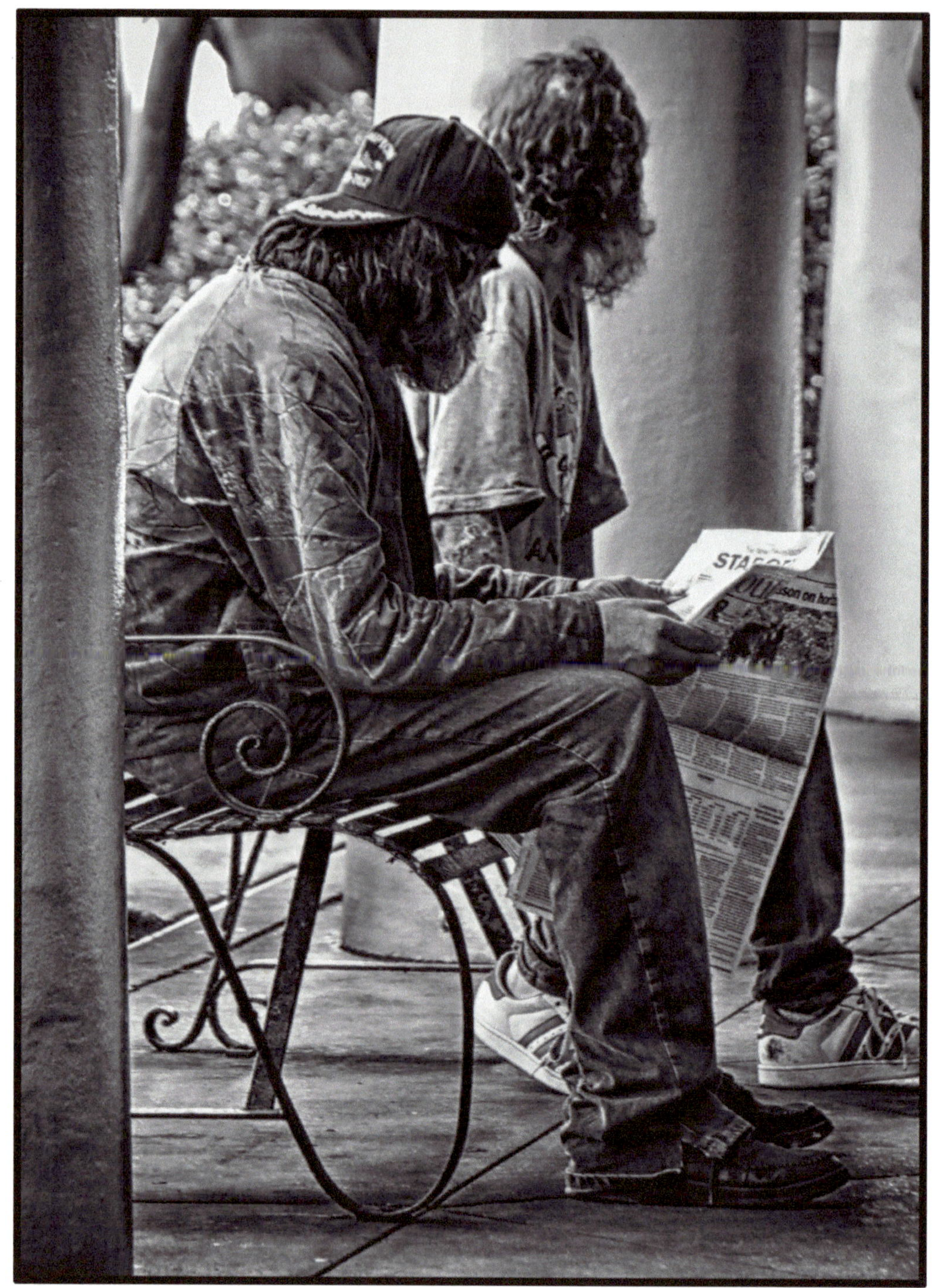

'Time To Spare'   Suzette McIntyre

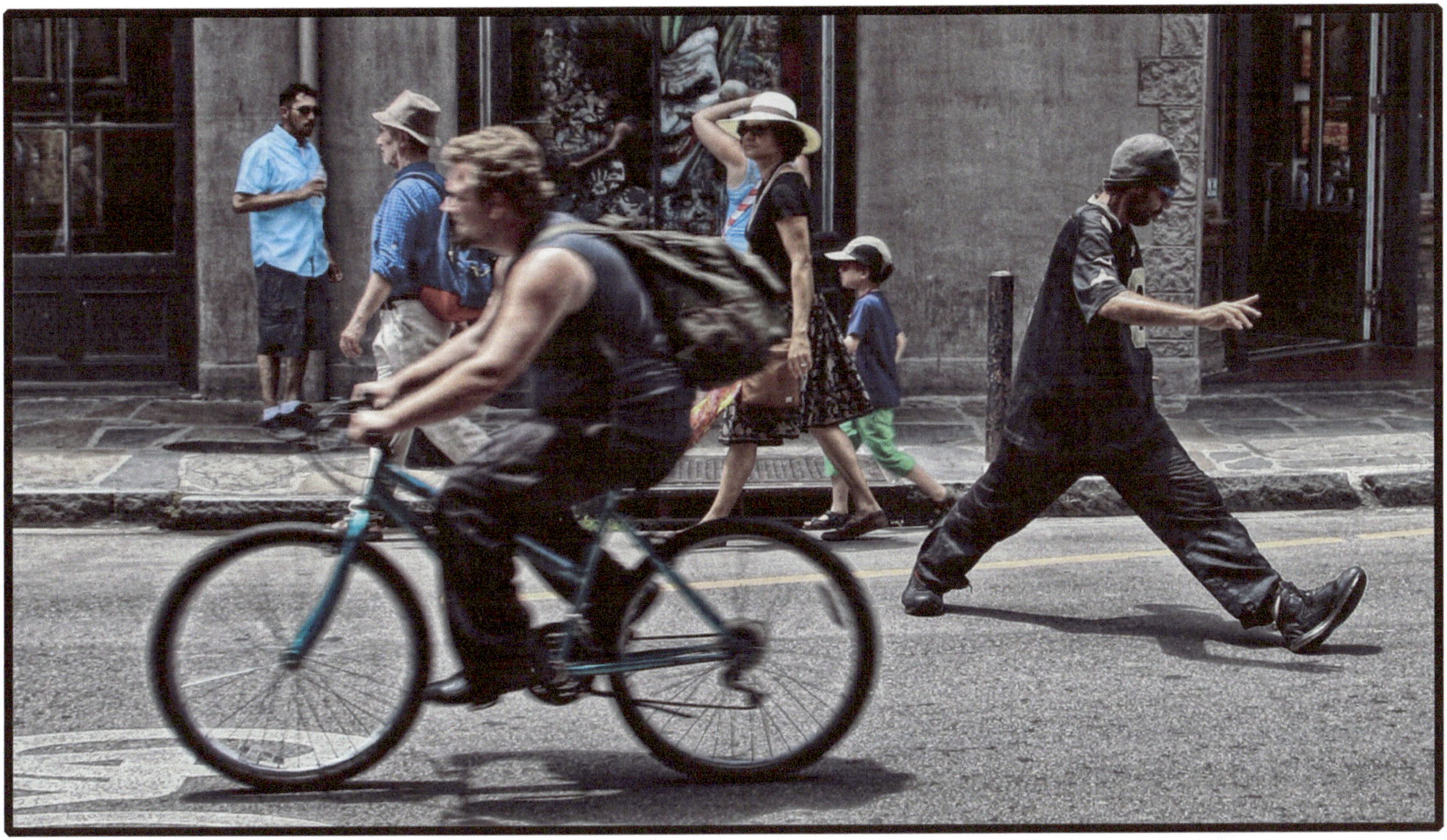

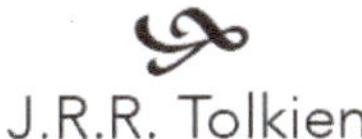

'Places To Go'   Suzette McIntyre

Not all who wander are lost.

J.R.R. Tolkien

Years later
I see clearly.
Stepping away from you
is where my road had dissappeared.

Lead me back.

~Suzette

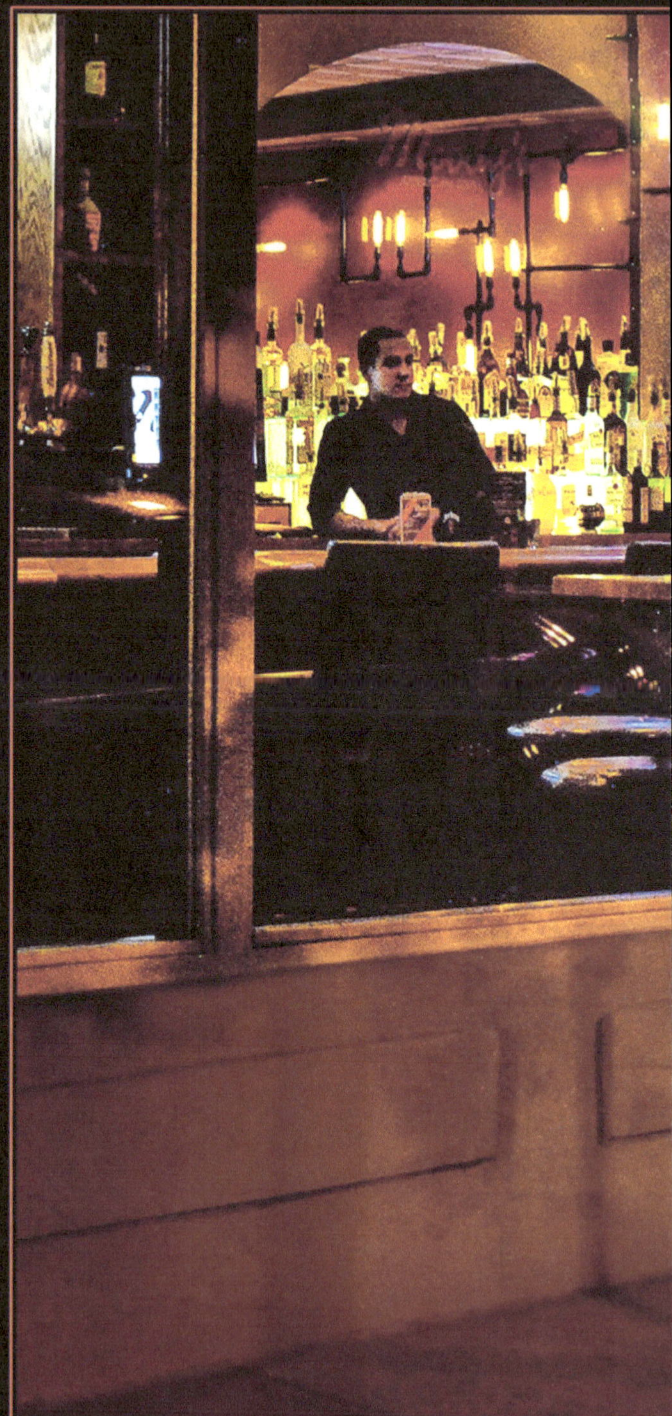

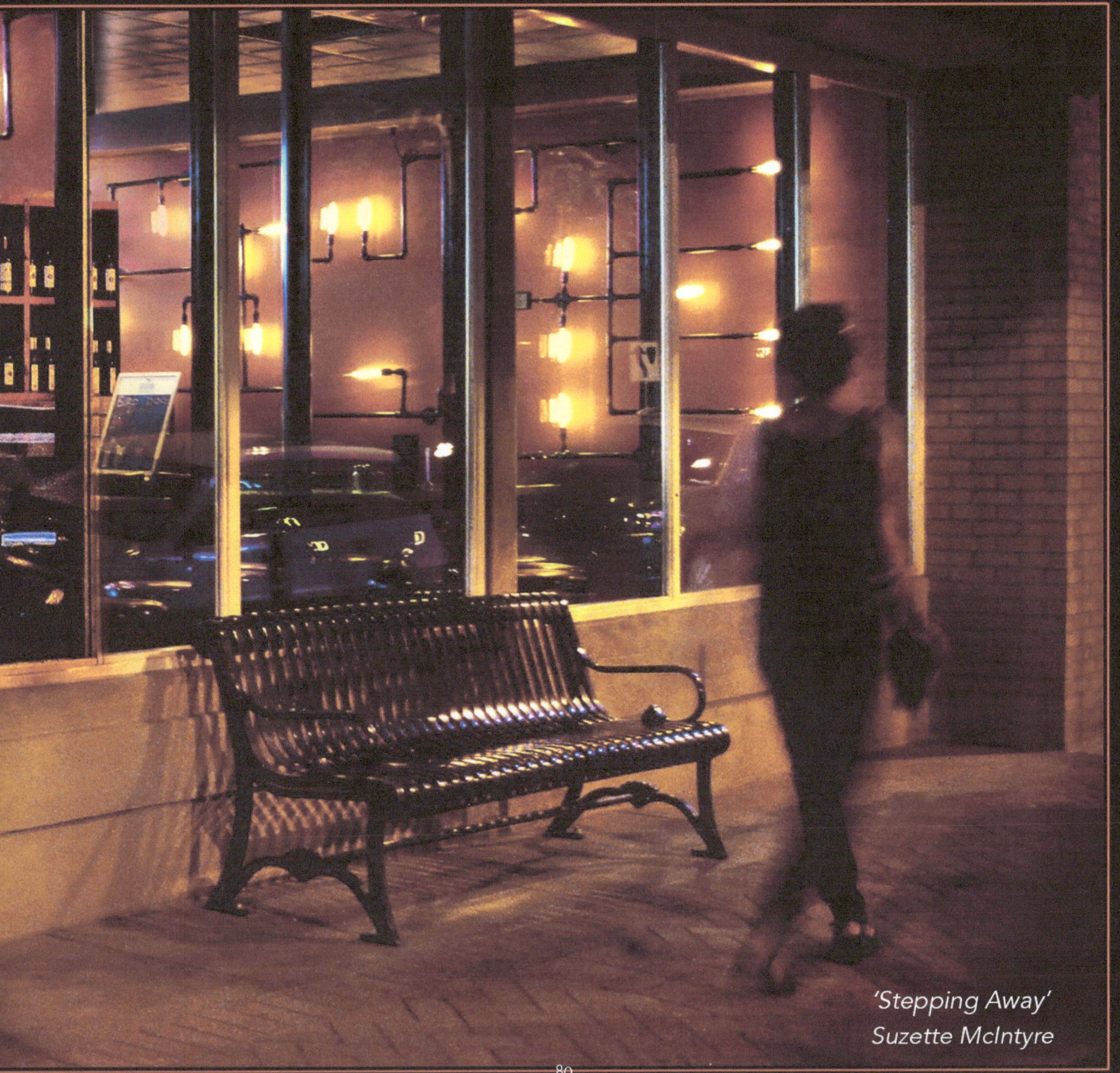

'Stepping Away'
Suzette McIntyre

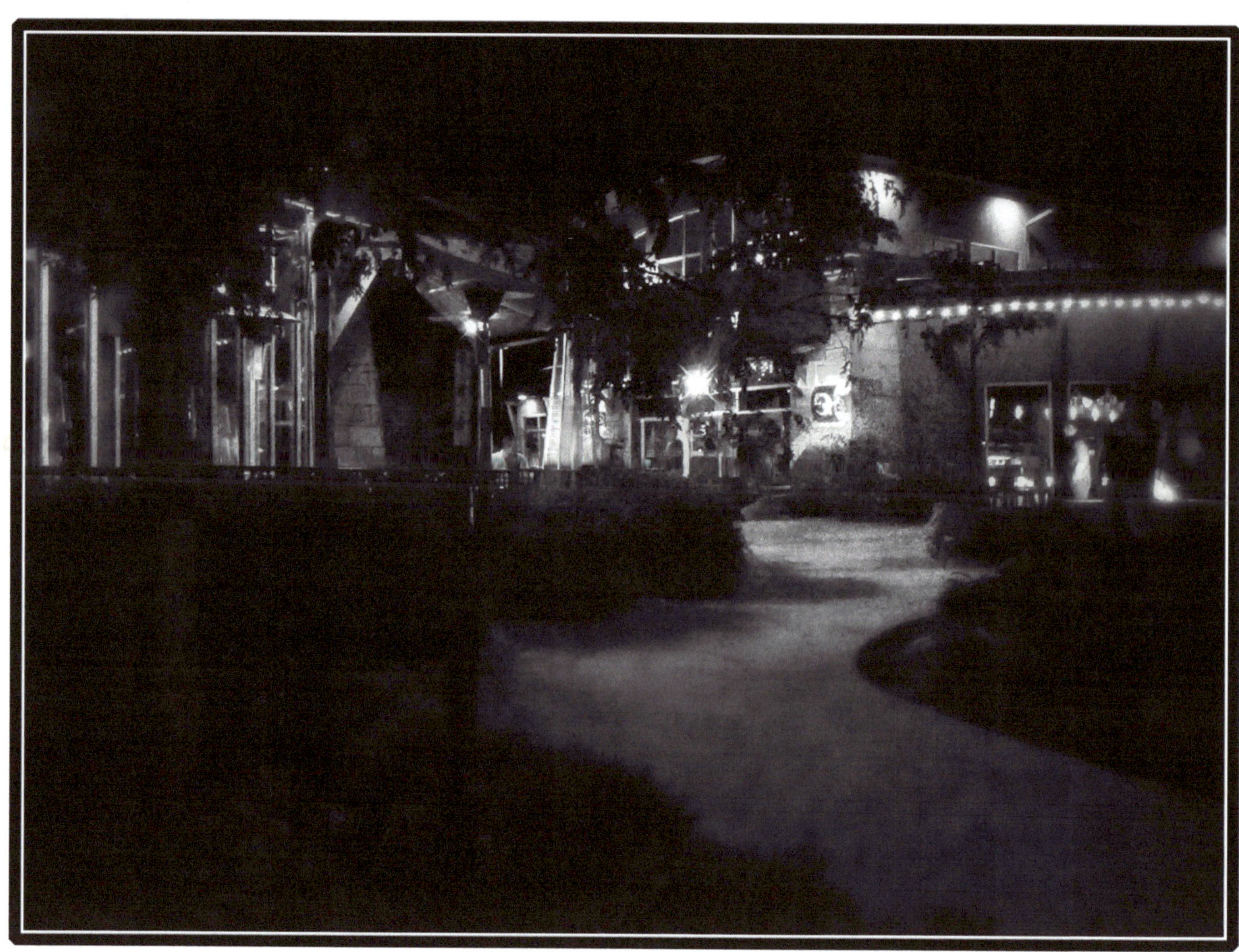

Stay the Course

As the night winds down
Ghostly images remain
Guiding us toward home

&

Kerrie Flanagan

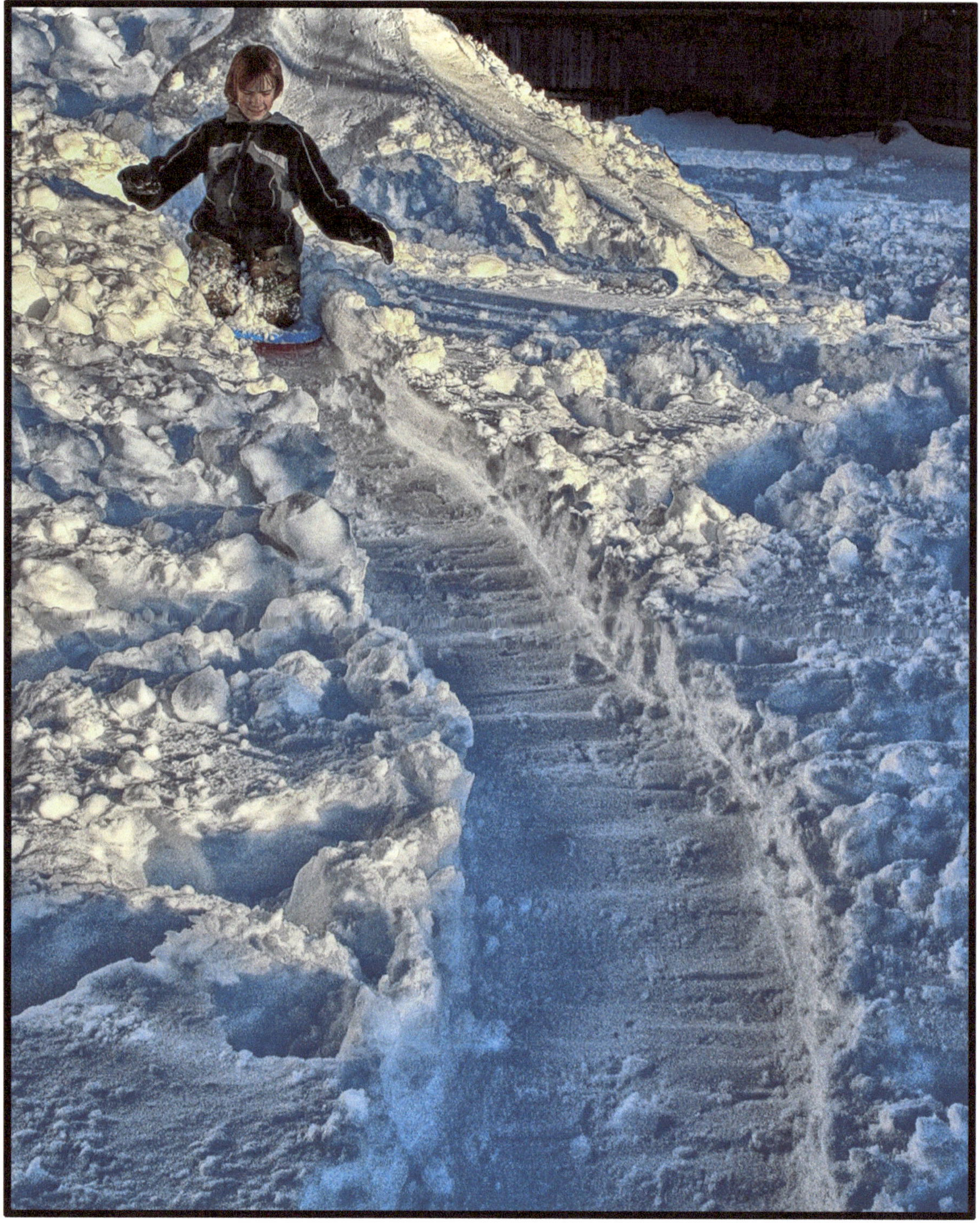

Your Path

Clean Slate
An idea sparks
Excitement slowly builds
Pushing to build something new
Celebrate!

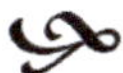

Kerrie Flanagan

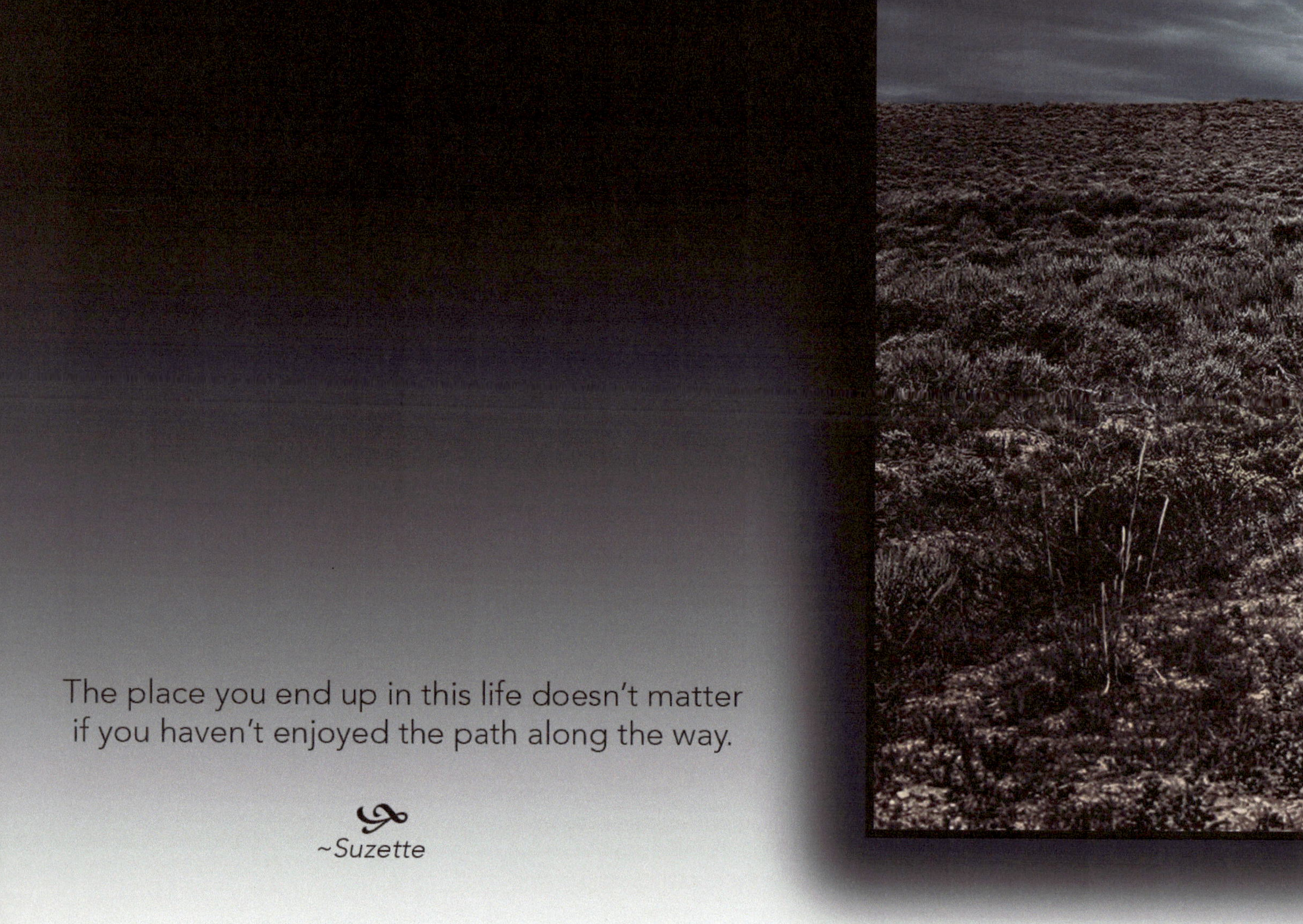

The place you end up in this life doesn't matter
if you haven't enjoyed the path along the way.

~Suzette

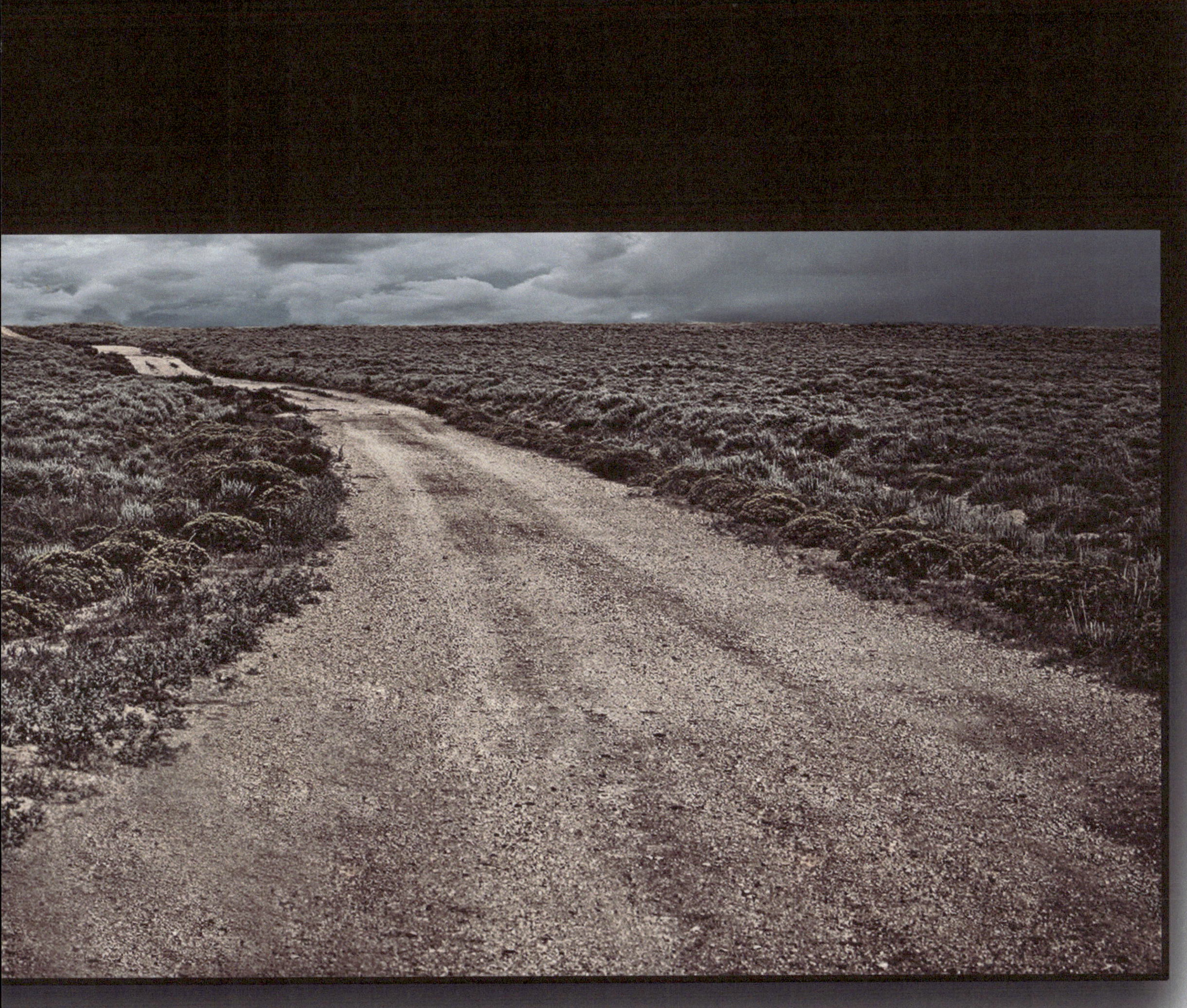

'Into the Storm'
Suzette McIntyre

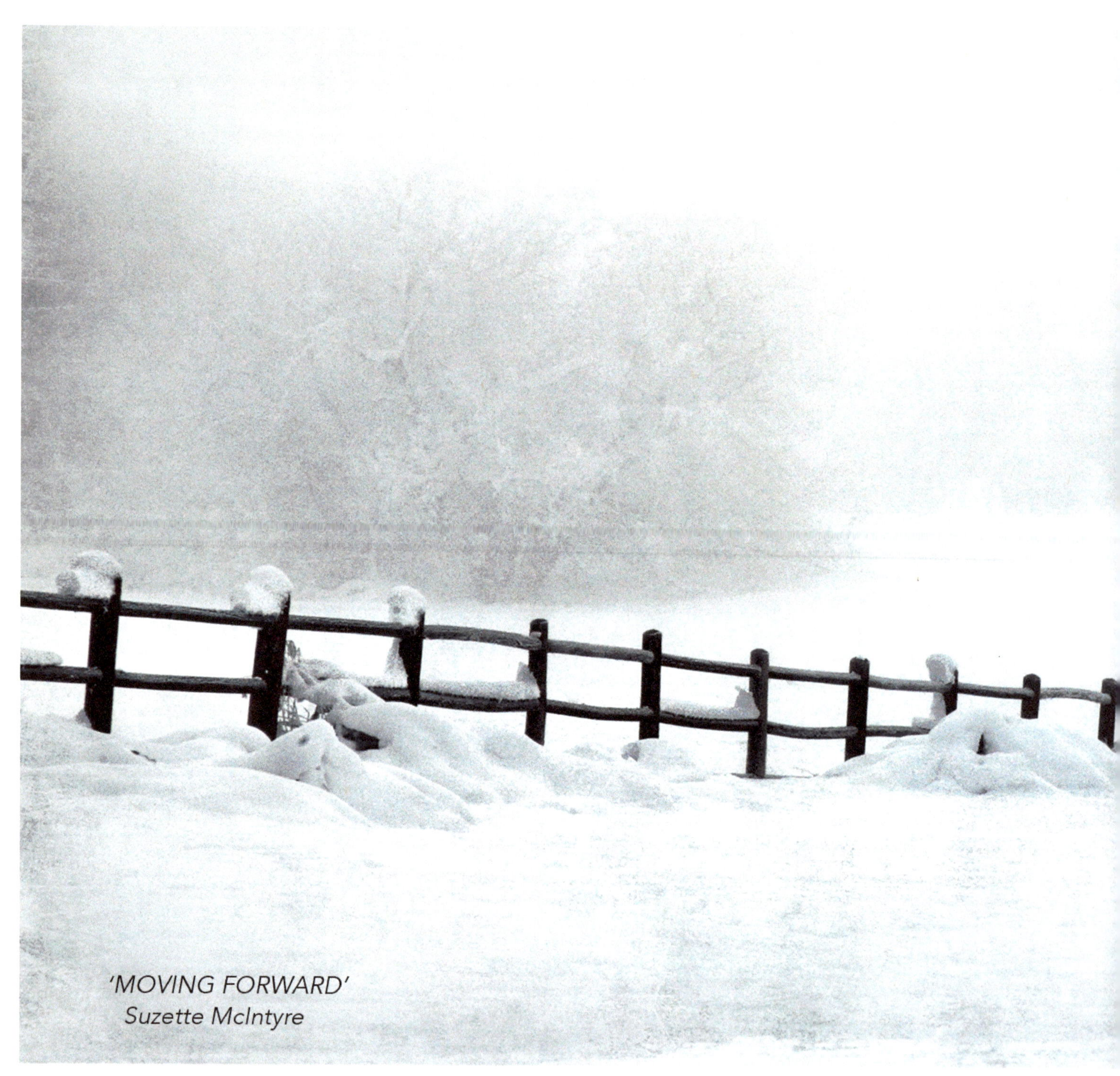

'MOVING FORWARD'
Suzette McIntyre

"Time stays long enough for anyone who will use it. "- Leonardo da Vinci

"What is not started today is never finished tomorrow." - Johann Wolfgang von Goethe

"Shun idleness. It is a rust that attaches itself to the most brilliant metals. "-Voltaire

"The world turns aside to let any man pass who knows where he is going." ~ Epictetus

"Why do you stay in prison when the door is so wide open?" ~Rumi

"Don't look where you fall, but where you slipped." African Proverb

"The journey is the reward." ~Taoist Proverb

"Freedom lies in being bold" ~Robert Frost

"My life is my message." ~Mahatma Ghandi

"Every wall is a door." ~ Emerson

"Courage is knowing what not to fear." ~Plato

"Don't let making a living prevent you from making a life." ~John Wooden

"You will either step forward into growth or you will step back into safety. " ~ Abraham Maslow

"Don't let yesterday take up too much of today." ~Will Rogers

"You will never reach your destination if you stop and throw stones at every dog that barks"
~WInston Churchill

"Between the head and feet of any given person is a billion miles of unexplored wilderness. "
~ Gabrielle Roth

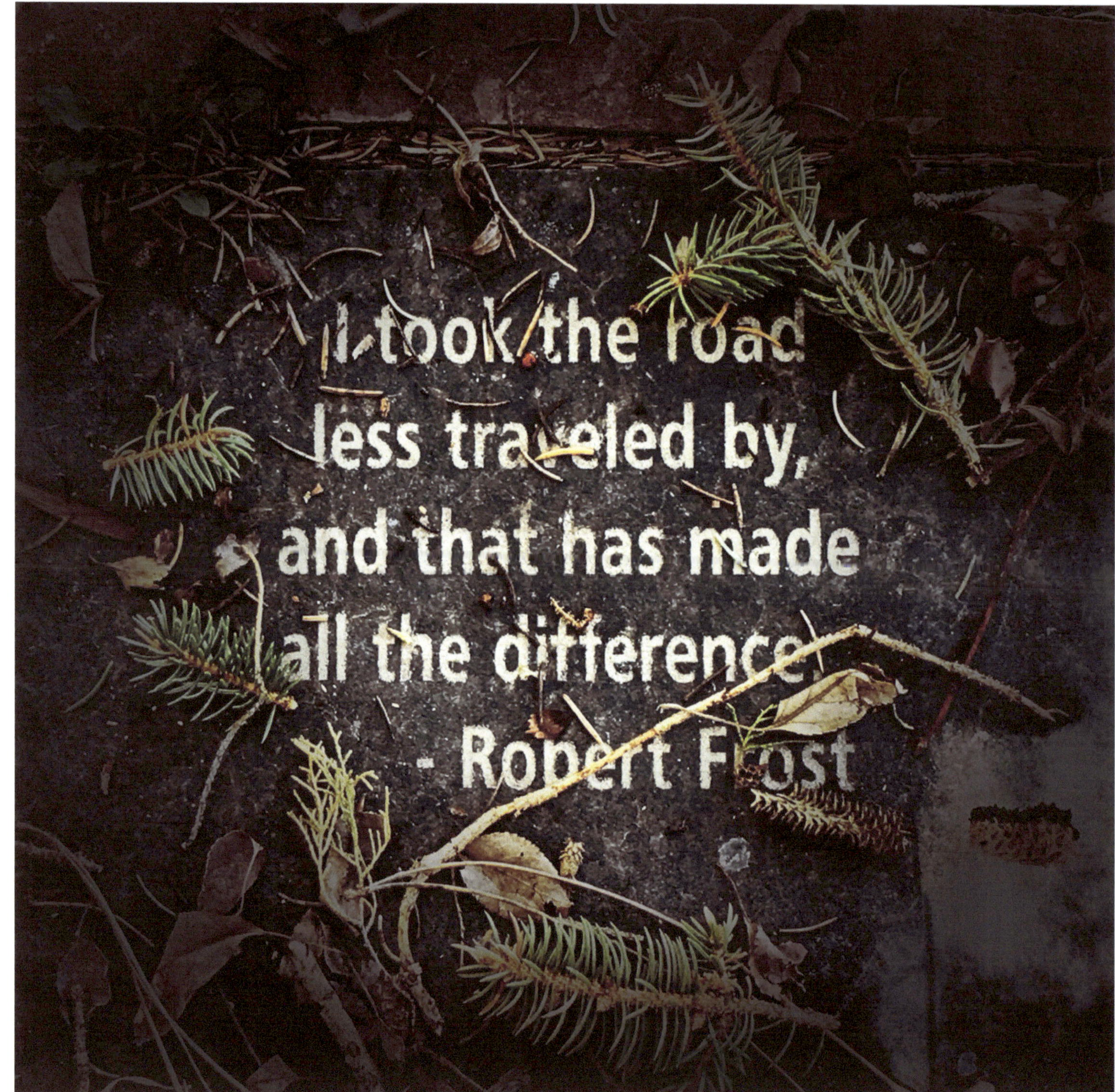

'A STONE IN THE PATH'

Suzette McIntyre

THE ROAD NOT TAKEN

Two roads diverged in a yellow wood,
And sorry I could not travel both
And be one traveler, long I stood
And looked down one as far as I could
To where it bent in the undergrowth;

Then took the other, as just as fair,
And having perhaps the better claim,
Because it was grassy and wanted wear;
Though as for that the passing there
Had worn them really about the same,

And both that morning equally lay
In leaves no step had trodden black.
Oh, I kept the first for another day!
Yet knowing how way leads on to way,
I doubted if I should ever come back.

I shall be telling this with a sigh
Somewhere ages and ages hence:
Two roads diverged in a wood, and I—
I took the one less traveled by,
And that has made all the difference.

~Robert Frost

ABOUT THE COMPETITION

THE GUEST ARTISTS & POETS featured in this edition are the winners of our second
'Words & Images' competition which was inspired by Robert Frost's Poem, 'The Road Not Taken'.

It is our desire to highlight and promote some of the incredible talent in this region
by featuring exceptional work in our book, so we called to artists for their interpretations
of Frost's poem with a slight twist: 'The Paths We Take'. In response to this call, the gallery
received over 200 entries. 100 pieces were juried in to compete.

The Jurors for this competition were meticulously selected, based on credentials and strengths
in their respective mediums. They spent hours scrutinizing these 100 juried pieces and chose
a 1st place, 2nd place, and 3 Honorable Mentions in each category: Photography, Painting,
Mixed Media and Poetry.

We appreciate your support of the arts!
~Suzette & Kerrie

COMPETITION JURORS

LISA ZIMMERMAN is an associate professor of English at the University of
Northern Colorado. She is a Phi Beta Kappa graduate in English and
History from Colorado State University and received her MFA in Creative
Writing from Washington University in St. Louis.

Her poetry and short fiction have appeared in anthologies as well as magazines
including Cave Wall, Florida Review, Poet Lore, Colorado Review, The Sun,
Natural Bridge, and Indiana Review, among other journals, and is the winner of
Redbook Magazine's Short Story contest.

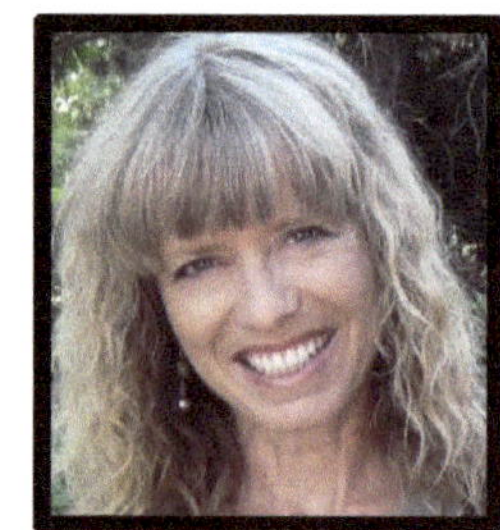

Lisa Zimmerman,
Poetry Judge

She is the author of five poetry collections including The Light at the Edge of
Everything (Anhinga Press 2008) and Snack Size: Poems (Mello Press 2012).
Her poetry has been nominated four times for the Pushcart Prize.

Lisa is a coach for the Poetry Out Loud high school recitation project and has taught writing workshops in K-12
classrooms in Colorado and Florida. She has been the poet-in-residence at schools in Fort Collins, Brighton,
Aurora, Idalia, and Longmont, and has been a master teaching artist at the annual Aesthetic Education Institute
of Colorado/Institute for Creative Teaching at the University of Denver 6 times. She lives in north Fort Collins
with her family.

SUSAN NELSON'S current work focuses on public art murals, collage portraits, and macro photography. However, Nelson's journey in the arts includes many map dots. She was involved with the founding of the Greeley Creative District and currently serves as Vice Chair of its Board. She was Director of Arts Marketing and Community Relations for the University of Northern Colorado's College of Performing and Visual Arts for 25 years, where under her direction, the College's promotional materials won several national awards. Prior to joining the Arts College at UNC, Nelson was executive director of the Community Center for the Creative Arts in Greeley, and taught drawing at Aims Community College.

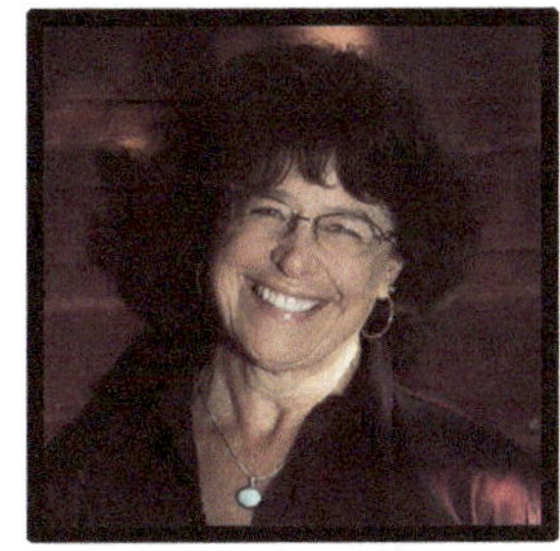

Susan Nelson,
Competition Judge

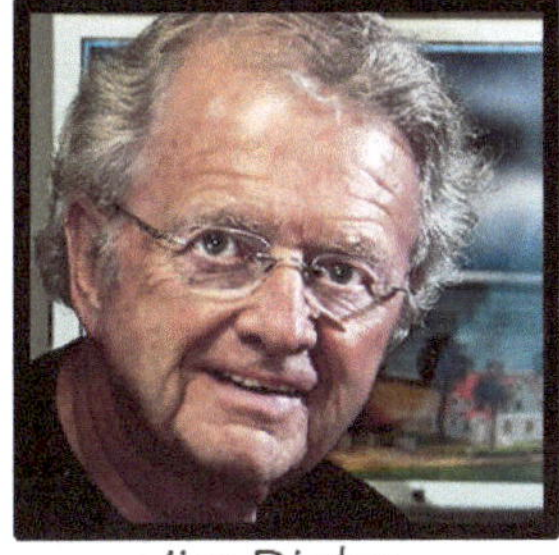

Her own artwork includes photography, drawing, pastels, collage and hand-made paper. She is also a published poet.

Nelson says, "I have worn many favorite hats, from artist to arts advocate to art classes, I've been engaged as a creator, teacher, manager, promoter and cheerleader for community access, learning and participation across the arts disciplines."

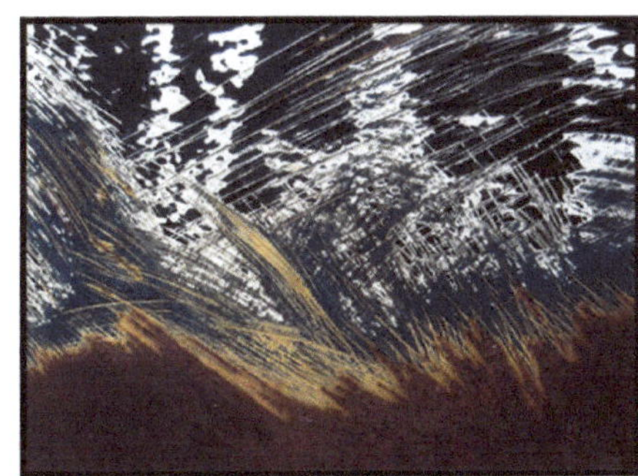

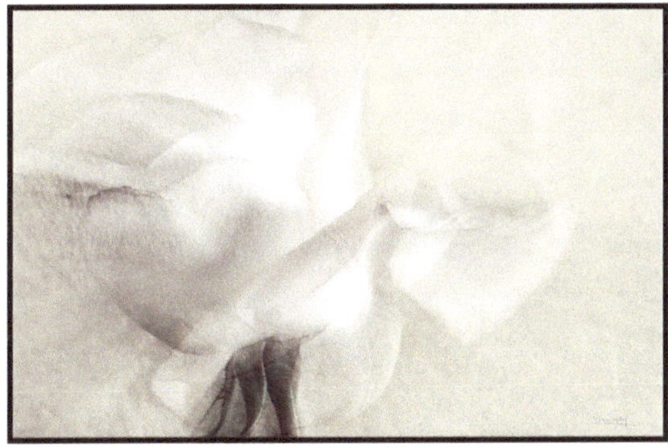

JIM DIGBY is a Colorado native and graduate of Brooks Institute of Photography. He has worked in still and motion picture photography since the late 1950's. His images have appeared on television and in magazines, including Life, National Geographic, Arizona Highways and Outdoor.

Jim Digby,
Competition Judge

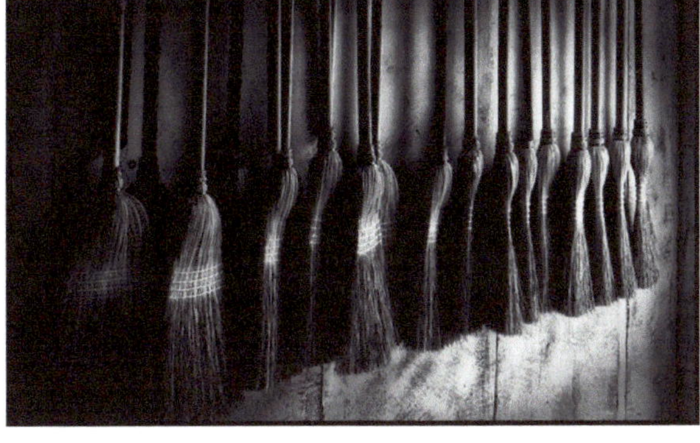

Digby has worked for Kodak, the National Center for Atmospheric Research, Martin-Marietta Corp, and The U.S. Bureau of Reclamation. His work has been exhibited in the U.S., Canada, Europe and Australia. An award winning photographer, Jim now specializes in fine art & product photography. He uses a technique he calls 'Optical Extraction' to capture details of natural and man made beauty. Jim & his wife Nancy enjoy life in Larimer County, Colorado.

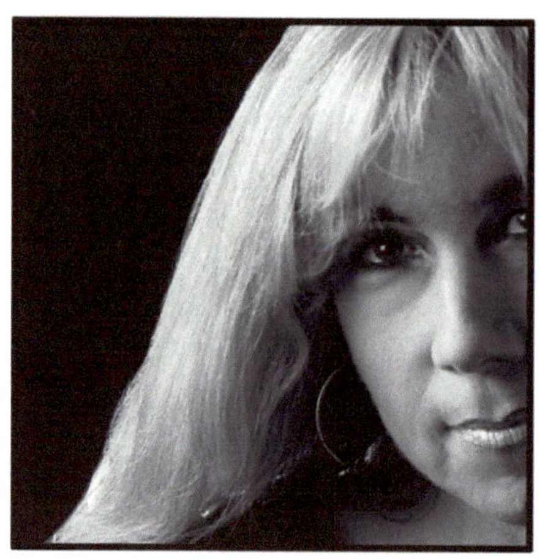

Suzette McIntyre,
Author, 'The Paths We Take'

*Suzette McIntyre is an award-winning artist and has been rec-
ognized internationally for her signature
style of photography and mixed media paintings.*

*She works in genres from weddings and portraiture,
to landscape and fine art.*

*Suzette views photography as a relationship
as well as an art, and combining the two creates
her intimate distinctive style.*

*Her canvases and photography, inspired by her
deep passion for people and her love of the western
wilderness can be seen in galleries throughout
Colorado and Wyoming and on her website:
http://www.PhotographyBySuzette.com*

*Suzette owns also owns Boardwalk Gallery and is the co-found-
er of Words & Images. She conducts regional juried art com-
petitions and the winners are published
in an accompanying coffee table book, as seen in this edition.*

*For more information about these competitions
log on to http://www.BoardwalkGallery.net*

Kerrie Flanagan is an accomplished freelance writer with over 17 years' experience, a writing consultant, author, publisher and the founder and former Director of Northern Colorado Writers.

Her recent articles are found in The Writer, Writer's Digest, Alaska Magazine, the Children's Writer's and Illustrator's Market and in the Writers Markets.

Her work appears in six Chicken Soup for the Soul books. She is the author of Planes, Trains and Chuck & Eddie; Claire's Unbearable Campout; Claire's Christmas Catastrophe and a co-author on Write Away: A Year of Musings and Motivations for Writers; and Beauty Surrounds Us; all published under her label Hot Chocolate Press.

In addition to her own work, she has helped nearly a dozen writers self-publish their work and has guided writers to reach their full potential. She teaches writing classes and presents at conferences throughout the U.S.

http://www.KerrieFlanagan.com
http://HotChocolatePress.com

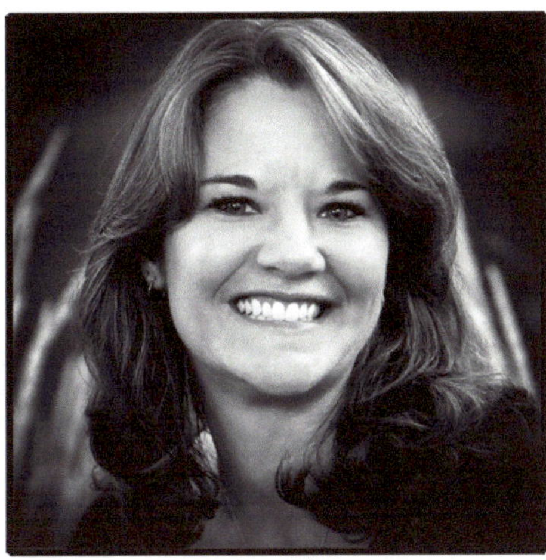

Kerrie Flanagan,
Author, 'The Paths We Take'

Printed in the United States of America
First Printing, 2016
Hot Chocolate Press
Fort Collins, Colorado

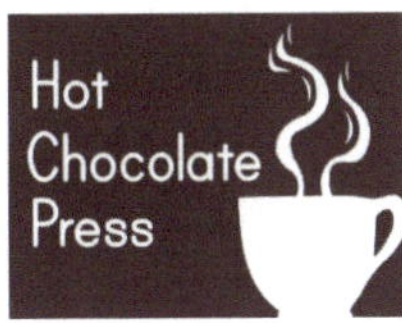

http://HotChocolatePress.com

Cover Design by Suzette McIntyre
with Photography By Suzette
www.photographybysuzette.com

ISBN-13:978-0-9961710-5-2

CPSIA information can be obtained
at www.ICGtesting.com
Printed in the USA
BVHW092139030820
585386BV00011B/85